Helen —
whose oe
lit my desire
and se foai.
Thank you.

JOURNEY
TO
GOD'S
HEART

Lois Caldwell
Prov 3: 5+6
Phil 4: 19

see page 130

TRUST IS BUILT, EYES ARE OPENED,
AND LIFE BECOMES A . . .

JOURNEY
TO
GOD'S
HEART

LOIS CALDWELL

WinePressPublishing
Great Books, Defined.

ISBN 13: 978-1-4141-2257-1
ISBN 10: 1-4141-2257-8
Library of Congress Catalog Card Number: 2011961014

To the two most important men in my life:
Jesus, my Savior and the lover of my soul,
and
Jim, my loving husband and fellow traveler on this journey,
without whom this never could have been written.

C ONTENTS

A Note to
the Reader

I love to tell the story,
'Twill be my theme in glory,
To tell the old, old story
Of Jesus and His love.
      —A. Catherine Hankey,
         "I Love to Tell the Story"

Remember the days of old;
    consider the generations long past.
Ask your father and he will tell you,
    your elders, and they will explain to you.
                —Deuteronomy 32:7

IT IS BEYOND doubt that I really do love to tell our story. And I always have had a propensity for asking the questions that others always wanted to ask but were hesitant, like "Where *do* you go when you follow Jesus?" This little epistle is the answer that unfolded as our family followed Jesus, and that journey is the story I love so much to tell.

I guess my greatest fear is that, when I enter the mansion which Jesus has prepared for me, this story will be forgotten. Like the apostle John, I suppose the world would not have room for all the books that could be written about all the things Jesus did. Nevertheless, I am adding to the great number which already exists, so our particular "days of old" might be remembered.

At a time when we were putting our children through college and paying for two weddings, my husband and I were asked by an investment salesman what our assets were. We had two used cars and no savings. I remember walking over to the china cabinet, where the pictures of our five children rested, and handing him their pictures. "These are our assets," I said.

He left shortly thereafter.

Since that time, I have come to realize that we have accrued another wonderful asset that our children will inherit, along with whatever amount of earthly goods we will leave. It is our story of where Jesus has taken us and how he managed to do it despite our misgivings, lack of faith at times, and serious doubts that we would always be able to follow.

So while I share this journey with all my readers, wherever you might be and whoever you are, this book is written especially with our children in mind. So now I address them, and the rest of you are invited to listen.

Dear Kathy, Bill, Sue, Nancy, and Dave,

This book is meant to be part of your inheritance, to be passed on to future generations. The other part of your inheritance is taken care of in our wills and most likely will vanish in a short time. This, however, is the part that will endure forever, for there is no undoing what is beyond explanation. Although it begs to be challenged, we have experienced it together and can say that it is truly so.

You'll recall that hymns have been a constant inspiration to Dad and me, so it shouldn't surprise you that every chapter begins with a portion of a hymn. You will also remember that Dad has been not only a Presbyterian pastor, but also a registered professional engineer. He long ago stopped trying to calculate the probabilities for circumstance when it came to how Jesus answered our prayers and provided at every turn of the road.

These experiences have left us with an unshakeable faith in God's care and provision. Our faith cannot be yours; neither can it be inherited. It can, however, be remembered and leaned upon so that the present seems not as scary and the future more sure.

No doubt there will be times in your lives when you wonder where God is, if he is even listening, or why things are happening that you cannot explain or do not want to happen. With the way situations are developing in the world today, there may even arise a time when the very core of your faith is challenged. In times like those, it will be good to consider what happened as we walked, questioned, struggled, and loved together. The care, the provision, the amazing obstacles that were overturned, and the fun and laughs we shared make up the wonderful story of how Jesus led our family straight to the heart of God—which is, after all, where you end up when you follow Jesus.

So, dear ones, enjoy reliving the good times we had together, the journey we were all part of, and the amazing love our Savior has for each of you. It is your inheritance for your children and their children, and it is for you to tell to anyone else who will listen.

All my love,

PROLOGUE
PREPARE YE THE WAY

How blessed are the children
Who in their parents see
The tender Father love of God,
And find their way to Thee.[1]
—Lois S. Johnson

**Hold onto instruction, do not let it go;
guard it well, for it is your life.**

—Proverbs 4:13

IT CERTAINLY WAS no accident that Jim and I landed where we did. God must have put a lot of forethought into how he laid his firm foundation, for there were a multitude of stones that were involved. The most noticeable were our parents.

Having a godly home is of no small consequence. Our home and family dinner table often were the site for entertaining visitors. In an era when discussing religion or politics with friends and acquaintances was viewed as just plain rude, it would seem that piece of etiquette left mighty little room for God to work. Yet the Christian instruction my siblings and I received practically leapt at us. The everyday example before us seeped into the very marrow of our souls and flowed through our beings.

My mother and father had come through the Depression. They had started married life and opened Dad's dental office when people were paying dental bills with smiles that had just been corrected, rather than with money. Just as they were beginning to "make it," Mom had a series of three miscarriages and Dad's loans, for dental school and his office equipment, began to come due.

Three children later, while they were still behind the eight ball financially, Mom was told she would have to abort the baby she was then carrying, because her life was in grave danger if she carried to full term. Of course, there was no health insurance in those days. Doctors and hospitals balked at getting paid in smiles, and Dad and Mom had to make a hard decision: leave three children motherless and incur outlandish medical bills, or abort the baby.

I was only eight years old at the time, but I remember being taken to see the operetta, *The Student Prince*. Dad thought it would get Mom's mind off the next day's dreaded abortion—to which they had reluctantly agreed, under great medical persuasion.

Mom had been left without a mother at the age of six, and she dreaded the possibility of us going through life without the love and wisdom that a mother can provide. She knew how lonely and lacking her own life had been. There was not much choice in light of what the doctors had predicted, but oh!—how she hated the whole prospect, which went against her deep love for children and everything she and Dad believed.

The musical production absolutely transported me to another world. Even so, I couldn't help wondering why my mother was weeping through what should have been, to my eight-year-old thinking, the premier event in life.

The next day arrived, and off Mom went to the hospital, not sure she would ever return to her family. She simply left the outcome in the Lord's hands, and she surrendered herself and the unborn baby into his capable care. What actually transpired could have been conceived only by God. Just as surgery was to begin, Mom, who had been in no danger of heart problems, had a heart attack on the operating room table! Surgery was cancelled immediately, and Mom was sent home to recover and face her demise when the baby would be born. She was overwhelmingly thankful for the way God had taken things into his own hands.

However, there were dark days ahead, so she spent those remaining months preparing us to face a motherless future. There was no extended family to care for us, and Dad would have to spend his days and evenings in the office. It seems strange to reflect upon now, but in those days dentists had both day and evening hours, and their work week was six days.

Every night, Mom sang to us while she rocked my little brother, Allen, to sleep. Trying to prepare us for life without her, she would remind us that we would always have each other and that Jesus would always be with us. Of course, I didn't take it too seriously. After all, life without a mother didn't compute.

What *did* compute were the words of the songs I heard over and over: "And He walks with me, and He talks with me, / And He tells me I am His own"[2] and "Let the lower lights be burning! / Send a gleam across the wave! / Some poor fainting, struggling seaman / You may rescue, you may save."[3] I didn't question their meaning. After all, if my mother said so, and kept repeating it night after night in her soft mezzo soprano voice, who was I to question? Jesus could and would walk and talk with me. I trusted that, and it was settled. I talked with Jesus and he talked right back. (So much for the idea that one has to pray "the sinner's prayer" to come to Jesus!)

In my candid conversations with Jesus, when I'd been put to bed and the lights were out, he somehow reminded me of my many misdemeanors and prevarications. With a smile I never saw but knew was there, he would accept my "sorry" and forgive me yet again, and I'd start the next day with a clean slate and no lingering shame.

As for hearing about the poor fainting and struggling ones who needed saving, it doesn't take a rocket scientist to see the influence on my elder sister and me and the resulting interests we share today. Carol was a founder of the Northwest Philadelphia Interfaith Hospitality Network, an outreach to the homeless, and I have shared my husband's ministry and work for foreign missions for the last thirty-five years. Jim and I now serve on the staff of World Mission Initiative, helping churches all over the USA to vitalize their mission programs, using what we learned by leading mission teams to fourteen countries around the world (but that comes later).

Mom survived, and I have a very wonderful brother, Bob, who would not have been born but for the grace of God through a heart attack at the right time.

With four children and debts they still had not been able to pay off, but with their faith in God, Mom and Dad went marching into the future. We had the delightful experience of never knowing we were not wealthy, for somehow we never wanted for the basics, and life was always an exciting adventure.

When we outgrew our house, moving to a new home meant a hefty mortgage and setting up a new office and patient base. Mom dubbed the new edifice "Mortgage Mansion," and the hours we spent painting and repairing would teach us that hard work was a part of doing what both Mom and the Lord required.

Of course, as we hung out the windows, painting and calling back and forth to one another, we furnished unexpected free entertainment for our rather starched neighbors. But truly we learned the value of a merry heart, for even in those teenage years we could see the humor in our antics and learned early to laugh at ourselves—another way of seeing the value in God's instruction to not think too highly of ourselves.

Dad, in his quiet, steady way, was another foundation stone on which we were being built. We were rather young when we realized that there was more to life than what one can accumulate. It was Dad's policy not to raise his fees when he knew times were lean for his patients; neither would he push for payment from people who could not afford dental care. This, it seemed, was just another opportunity to trust the Lord and a challenge for how to meet our own pressing needs. More than once, as he entered his office on the side of our home, it was with a prayer that the patients would be able to pay this time.

Surprisingly, I don't remember a single time that patients' payments did not meet our needs. There were never lectures about cause and effect, just the picture of faith and prayer at work. Integrity, faithfulness, and compassion seemed to have something to do with fatherhood, both Dad's and the Father whom he obviously served.

Mom, who had returned to teaching to help with the needs of a growing family and future college educations, had the curious habit of every once in a while bringing home for dinner a needy person she had met. We were never quite sure who the extra person was at our table and quickly learned not to ask, but just to adjust the portions so there was enough for all. Oh, we watched Mom's concern when the bills stacked up, even when she once pawned her engagement ring, but somehow that never translated into worry. By the end of her life, we better understood her and a little more about walking with her Savior.

Her bout with breast cancer was Mom's final legacy to us, for both her girls have faced the same challenge. Three weeks before she died, she smilingly told me, "Oh, don't worry about me. I really can't wait to get rid of this body." Then she added, "And don't you girls dare wear black to my funeral!" When we saw each other at the funeral, Carol and I both laughed. We were both wearing white! The foundation had been laid: we knew whom to trust, to whom we all belonged, and where we were all going.

God quarries his foundation blocks in different places and brings them together in quite unorthodox ways. Jim and I met in first grade. He was not exactly enamored about a girl a head taller than he was and even less so when her father became his family's dentist. Not only were those strikes against any future together, but I could easily level him, and he knew it.

The feeling of distaste was quite mutual, because the academic competition between us was fierce. However, our mothers became friends, and that resulted in my being invited to all of Jim's birthday parties. Imagine having to give presents to someone whose every party resulted in coming away with the fear that your behavior would be the topic of conversation between your mother and his—and the consequences!

Yet the eyes of God see far into the future. After fifth grade, my family moved away to our "Mortgage Mansion," and Jim and I would not see each other until my senior year in college—except once, when his mother dragged him along on a visit, and my hasty retreat upstairs saved me from having to be sociable toward him.

What my eyes did not see was the training that was going on in the Caldwell household. As in my home, there was not overt teaching, but always an example being set. Attendance at church and giving for the work of the kingdom of God were not options, swearing was frowned upon, and dishonest and unkind behaviors were not tolerated. Money was appreciated as a means of support rather than something to be used for luxuries, and drinking anything alcoholic was out of the question, as in our home.

Dad Caldwell was a model gentleman and taught his sons the value of manners, patience, faithfulness, and dependability. His was a graphic illustration of how a father provides for those in his care, a lesson not difficult to translate into understanding how our heavenly Father meets our every need.

Mother Caldwell had overcome the hardships of being sent away from her mother at six years old. Her father had died before she was born, leaving an immigrant mother alone in a strange country with a young child needing to be cared for and supported. Mother Caldwell had longed for a higher education, and she saw to it that her two sons would not only go to college but excel. Both graduated as engineers, one going on to his master's degree in that field and the other eventually to seminary.

Education, however, was not the only priority. Attendance at Sunday school began for the boys at age three, and it was she who took thirteen-year-old Jim off to revival meetings and encouraged him to go forward and give his life to the Lord. While all of this was being carefully orchestrated by the Lord, there were the usual tiffs and struggles that can result when two boys of different temperaments grow up in a household together, yet the moral character of the Caldwell boys was being molded and shaped for use in God's kingdom.

When Jim and I reconnected ten years later, at a Drexel University dance, it was no wonder we stood gaping at each other. Jim was now six feet tall and a handsome knight—or so he appeared to a short, petite girl who was sure that Miracle-Gro had been included in his diet. Jim was equally nonplussed, wondering what had happened to the Amazon with long red curls. God must have had a good chuckle!

With the bottom tier of the foundation in place, there were layers of education and church that followed. Both of us attended public school and heard Bible reading and prayer every morning during the opening exercises that began every school day. While great spiritual insights did not occur because of this, I am repeatedly amazed at how, while wishing to "get it over with," much was absorbed. At least that atmosphere was a comfortable and reliably sure place to grow. Twelve years of hearing a psalm or other Old Testament reading every morning of your school career surely gives some direction for behavior and morality, a resting place of comfort, and some familiarization with what God might require of your life.

It was in Beaver College, a Presbyterian college where Bible courses and chapel attendance were required in those years, that I came head-on with questions that would set me looking for something more. The Lord had created me with an insatiable curiosity and courage to ask questions. Ask I did; unfortunately,

I didn't get answers. Maybe it was a case of "he who has ears, let him hear" (Matt. 13:43), but I think not, for I distinctly remember being told that my faith was too simplistic.

Fortunately, the library and I were good friends, and we were about to become better acquainted. I began to read the Christian classics, including *Foxe's Book of Martyrs*. The more I read, the simpler it appeared to me: believe and trust in Jesus Christ as Savior and Lord, and God will direct your paths. That fact actually had been settled long before, but there was one question which still bothered me: if I were faced with the choice between torture—or even death—and acknowledging my Savior, as were the people I was reading about, how long would it be before I betrayed him?

There would be more to the search before everything fell into place.

After graduation, and then a year of teaching while Jim finished his five-year engineering course, the knight and the petite redhead were married. The knight looked even more handsome in his uniform, and the Army's claim on Jim took us to Germany.

Four thousand miles from home, before e-mail, the nine-dollar-per-minute rate for an overseas phone call rather restricted the influences of family and the warm connections that had been so familiar. We grew to depend on each other in an atmosphere that did not exactly endorse the moral code we both had inherited and now firmly believed in. God's shaping for the way we would walk later was starting to be apparent. We would see divorce and decide it was not in our vocabulary. Integrity and honesty were non-negotiable and unfaithfulness not acceptable. Being true to what we had been taught made us very aware that our parents' examples had taken root.

Discouraged with what I was seeing as "church," I announced that perhaps God and I would continue our relationship without my leading the chapel choir and my attendance at services. The chapel had once been the war room of a German SS regiment, and walking down the aisle over the large inlaid tile swastikas did not exactly help my sagging attitude.

Enter the knight in his Army uniform, backed up by his strong sense of discipline and obedience to what God requires. Jim insisted that we continue to go to church. Maybe it was not the ultimate example of submitting to one's husband, but I shudder to think about where our relationship with God would be today if we had not walked together.

This difference of opinion opened up lively and sometimes heated discussions between us, often extending into the wee hours of the morning. Jim insisted that only obedience mattered. I thought he was too rooted in Old Testament law, insisting that one's obedience grew as a result of love. He thought I had spent too much time reading the gospel of John. It would be awhile before we could put it all together.

The Berlin Wall went up, we marveled that something did not set off a nuclear disaster, and our three-year tour in Germany was extended for six additional months. It was our first time to face the serious possibility that there might be a time when Jim would be in danger, and I might have to leave all of our possessions and flee. Those thoughts did not sit at all comfortably with me. Not seeing into the future, it never occurred to me that this was preparation for future mission work—where *things* would take a back seat to sharing the gospel, and going would be where the Lord led.

Kathy, our eldest, put in her appearance, which ended my teaching career at the American Military School in Nürnberg. Now responsible for someone other than ourselves, we became aware that we really did not want a life of danger, separation, and sending children off to boarding school in a foreign country. It seemed that our feet were being directed to follow a different fork in the road.

Jim resigned his Regular Army commission and resumed his engineering career, although both of us regretted leaving a career that had given such a sense of purpose and high calling, as well as the tight and supportive community life to which we had become accustomed. In future years, it was the latter we would hunger for in the Christian community, but very rarely have we found it to the extent we experienced it in military life.

As four more children were added to the family, life took on a certain predictability. Church life ballooned into leading the children's choir, writing a new Sunday school program, and Jim taking on Sunday school superintendent and deacon responsibilities. Although we heard the Word clearly preached at the Presbyterian church we attended, there was always a feeling that something was missing, some spark of life that we could not find.

Our friends were less than receptive to hearing anything that would have caused them to ponder thoughts about God being the maker of the universe, let alone the master of their lives. Being the more detailed, factual person, Jim decided to use archeology to prove the truth of the Bible to them, and in the process discovered that he was trying to prove it to himself! Providentially, no sooner did he find something convincing, than something else would be published that was counter to it. It was a good lesson in the need to believe, without man-made proof, in the God who transcends logic.

Jim settled the issue for himself; the only means for believing the veracity of God's Word, he decided, was simply to just believe! So, in his straightforward way, he made the choice to believe, then and forever. And that was that; no ifs, buts, or struggling with questions. It was a matter of faith—choosing to be sure of what he hoped for and certain of what he could not see.

No wonder, when someone asked the question, "What are you doing with your Christianity?" that we began to wonder exactly what we *were* doing with our Christianity. Our uneasiness increased as we followed our pastor's suggestion that the congregation not fast for Lent, but instead feast on the Word of God by reading through the entire New Testament in those forty days. Being tired after chasing five little children around all day, and Jim being sleepy after hours of design and desk work, we hit on a plan to read through the New Testament together: he would wash the dishes after the children were in bed, while I sat on a stool in the kitchen and read it aloud.

When we reached the early chapters of Acts, one of us observed, "If *that* is living the Christian faith, then we are hardly scratching the surface—sort of like skating and hardly making a mark on the ice." This did nothing for relieving our discomfort level. It seemed that we were bumping into the same challenge wherever we turned!

To help the coffers, I had started to tutor. One day, when my student had to stay past his hour, his mother waited in the car in front of our house. I went to ask her if it would be all right to take a few more minutes to finish and, just as I reached her, a cloudburst sent me scurrying out of the rain into the shelter of her car. Just as I started to apologize for intruding, this woman—whom I hardly knew—threw down the book she had been reading onto the seat next to me, exclaiming, "I am *sick* of my Christian life!"

Now that is enough to startle anyone so, rain or not, I carefully edged toward the door, but not without glancing at the cover of the book that had produced such an outburst. The title seemed harmless enough, so without much delay, I bought a copy of the book and began to read of the recent revival in East Timor. I didn't immediately see the connection between what I was reading and the questions we were asking, but God knew the effect it would have in our lives. If God actually was doing the outlandish things I was reading about, even if they were happening halfway around the world, then perhaps there really *was* something we were missing. I began a serious search.

Some of the greatest events in life receive the least or worst reactions, and my search was about to be met by both. I went back to the library and began reading all of the church fathers' writings I could get my hands on. I read until my eyes crossed—and acquired quite a theological education. *Jonathan Edward's Collected Writings* still stands out as one of the driest tomes I have ever read, but along with Luther's, Augustine's, St. John of the Cross's, and a myriad of others' writings, something was beginning to emerge.

To make things more complicated, this was in the early 1970s, during the charismatic revival! I also was reading about present-day healings and about speaking in tongues and then finding references to such happenings in early church history. The result was profound: I was greatly confused! The pastor was no help, for he firmly believed that these out-of-the-ordinary things were not of God. That, I later realized, is exactly where God does his most amazing works—in out-of-the-ordinary places, in out-of-the-ordinary ways, with ordinary people.

I decided to get unconfused. I had read enough of man's works, so I decided to go back to reading what God had said. As I sat in bed one evening, with a concordance and my Bible, looking for I-didn't-know-what, I realized that I had put my trust in Scripture to supply the answers. Heartbroken at seeming to be no nearer to finding what I was seeking, I put down the Bible. As I did, it fell open, and through tears I read, "I have no greater joy than to hear that my children walk in truth" (3 John 4, KJV). With utter despair, I turned out the light and pleaded, "Then show me the truth!"

I cannot promise that anyone else will receive the answer I did, but God was waiting for me to ask at just that moment, in just that way, in just the state I was in. I had asked him to show me the truth, and he showed me himself! I saw Jesus, the living Lord! He actually appeared in the room, surrounded by light, and stood at the foot of my bed. Confusion fled out the window and awesome wonder replaced it.

On his command, after he disappeared, I cautiously woke Jim—expecting that if I related what had just happened, my husband would think me addled, if not downright deranged. I should have known that what God begins, he finishes with flourish.

Jim listened to my tale, believing every word as unquestionably true. (But then, this was the man who took things at face value and didn't question the Lord.) Now there was one more thing to discern: what did this mean for us, and why had it happened? The years ahead would answer those questions. God was uniquely preparing the way.

Very carefully, Jesus had created a sure path on which we could begin our journey to places we could never imagine—and ultimately to the destination God desires for all his children: his heart.

C H R I S T I A N , L O V E M E
M O R E T H A N T H E S E

Jesus calls us; o'er the tumult
 Of our life's wild, restless sea,
Day by day His sweet voice soundeth,
 Saying, "Christian, follow me."
    —Cecil F. Alexander

**"I know the plans I have for you," declares the LORD,
"plans to prosper you and not to harm you, plans
to give you hope and a future."**
    —Jeremiah 29:11

UNDOUBTEDLY IT WOULD have been easier if Jim and I had known where we were going. We had five others to think about, rather than just ourselves, and wherever we were headed, we were committed to going there as a family. I was fast acquiring a deep appreciation for Sarah packing her household belongings to go who-knows-where, to do who-knows-what, for who-knows-how-long! But at least she had known she was on the move. We didn't even know we actually had started.

We were seven in number and we were taking on the likeness of a parade. However, Jesus was well aware of that and, as master of ceremonies, was lining us up for the marching order. Now, if there is to be a parade, everyone involved needs to be in agreement and going in the same direction. Jesus had been working quietly behind the scenes so that we would all be of one accord, as we struck out on what would be a more amazing journey than any of us could have imagined.

All five children had come to know the Lord and had asked Jesus into their hearts. Bill, at seven years old, had prayed with me after settling some knotty questions. The year before, just as I had put him to bed one evening, he announced that he had finally figured out what sin was all about. I paused at the door, wondering what I was about to hear. Bill hurried to explain, before another "Go to sleep" could come his way. "It's just like you fell into a big black hole and you're hanging on to the edge. There's a big, ferocious lion at the bottom waiting to eat you up if you fall in" (this latter being said with accompanying growling and baring of teeth). "And just when you get tired and start to slip, there's a big hand that comes down and lifts you out. Isn't that right, Mommy?"

His explanation might never grace the pages of theological books, but it certainly captured the idea with amazing clarity. I wished that some other explanations I had heard were as insightful. Bill had settled the issue of sin and salvation, and it was not long until he reached for the Hand that would lift him up and carry him through life.

Now on a mission, Bill became our in-house evangelist. Shortly thereafter, Sue came to know her Healer. Nancy, who listened to Sue and Bill talk about the Lord and light up like light bulbs when they did, also decided that having the Lord in her life was a good idea. Being only fifteen months younger than Sue, Nancy thought anything Sue did was a good idea. But it was no wonder that accepting the Lord was appealing; when Sue was asked how she knew Jesus was in her heart, she smiled, her eyes danced, and in awed tones she answered, "Oh, Mommy, the glory!" That's a pretty good recommendation for anyone!

While Bill enjoyed his status as the only male surrounded by all of his sisters, and willingly was the "daddy" when they played house and had their tea parties, he truly wanted a brother. After the arrival of his third sister, Bill had started to pray for a brother and, out of compassion, Jim and I soon found ourselves asking the Lord, just as fervently, that Bill would have his desire. When we announced that another child was on the way, he began praying with such determination and persistence that Jim and I began to wonder what would happen to his fledgling faith if another girl were to be added to our family!

As we approached the baby's birth, with some trepidation I asked Bill what would happen if the baby turned out to be another sister. Bill just smiled and said, "Oh, that's OK, Mom. I'll just pray for another one to be a boy." Jim and I doubled our prayers—after all, five children would be more than enough! So it was that Dave entered the world. Bill was delighted, and we had learned a lesson in persistent faith, much like Jesus' parable of the woman who unfailingly kept petitioning the judge (Luke 18:1–8).

As soon as he perceived that Dave was old enough to understand the need for Jesus to be in one's life, Bill went right to work. In his eyes, age three was plenty old enough. It was not long until he had a big-brother talk with Dave about the Lord.

I never would have known what had transpired except I asked Dave one day, as mommies occasionally do, who loved him best of all. His immediate reply was "Jesus does!" After a few pangs of jealousy and readjusting my ego, I inquired how he knew that to be true. "Bill prayed with me in my crib," he answered matter-of-factly, as if making such momentous decisions was just part of the landscape. But then, maybe it *is* that simple when one comes as a little child. In fact, life really would be a lot less complicated if we all approached it with such trust and certainty. Surely, inauspicious beginnings don't seem to detract, for Dave's faith grew steadily from that acorn beginning to the oak-solid faith that sustains him today.

Kathy remained the only one outside the fold. As the eldest, she was not about to have her kid brother tell her what to do. After all, directing her siblings was the role of the big sister. She was listening, however, when we tuned into a TV broadcast of a Billy Graham Crusade some months later. As he always does, Reverend Graham left no doubt of the need for a Savior and of what happens to those who choose to reject him. Kathy, somewhat frightened at the proposition of spending a Christless eternity, asked us to pray with her as she asked Jesus to be her Savior and Lord. Right then, as we prayed together on the sofa, Kathy's future was secured.

While Kathy has always taken her relationship with the Lord very seriously, she also sees the fun in things. When asked to give her testimony, she has often confounded sober souls by declaring that, at the age of eleven, she had the hell scared out of her!

We were all marching in the same direction now. The parade could begin, although there was not much fanfare or accompanying music playing, unless the rejoicing in heaven counted. The Parade Master was out in front. Our task was to keep up with him—and that would be no small adventure!

Jim's career had embraced being the executive officer of a US Army armored engineer company in Germany, which entailed working with defense obstacle plans for protecting the border. After leaving the military, he had been responsible for high pressure equipment production. Both jobs had required the awareness that big things matter.

By now, though, Jim was designing punched card machines for computers, and the minutia of it all was getting to him. He was becoming more and more dissatisfied with his everyday existence, and his dissatisfaction was fast becoming mine. Curiously, there was no real reason for such discomfort. Jim's salary was sufficient to meet all of our needs, his commute was minimal, he was considered one of the top engineers in the company, and he was highly respected by all those who worked with him. But there he was, one unhappy man.

In frustration one evening, I asked Jim what he really desired to do, only to be told that he wanted to do whatever God directed. We were getting nowhere, so I blurted out, "Well, if God weren't in it, what would you want to do?" The further the conversation went, the more comical it became. Jim responded, "I'd really like to be a minister and do something that would affect people's lives, but you don't do that unless God calls you." I had to admit that he had me stumped there, for no sane person would venture down that path without God being in it!

To settle the issue once and for all, Jim decided to call a friend who had graduated with him from college, served in the Army, gone on to seminary and the ministry, had soon left the pastorate, and was again employed doing engineering. When Jim asked him how he had discerned God's call, our friend replied that it really was just a matter of making up your mind and pursuing what you wanted to do. Jim put down the phone and pronounced with finality, "That settles it. You don't go into the ministry unless you have a definite call. He wasn't called, and that's the reason he's no longer in the ministry. God's call is a must."

Jim wouldn't be leaving the engineering field anytime soon.

We had been urged by several friends to visit a large Presbyterian church nearby to hear the dynamic interim pastor there. As their requests became more frequent, we decided to pacify them one Sunday. We packed the troops into the car and took off to see what was so exciting. Frankly, we were sure there would not be much to stir our souls there, as this was *the* church in our area where the doctors, lawyers, and bankers attended and, in our thinking, God most likely did not.

Our family entered with the stir that accompanies trying to find seats for seven people together. As usual, we wound up sitting near the front of the church because we required an entire pew, and those were always available close to the chancel. We settled in and waited, somewhat skeptically, to see what God had in store.

It wasn't long until we realized that something very unexpected was happening. Somehow, the entire atmosphere had changed. Souls were being stirred, not the least of which were our own. The pastor finished his sermon, the last hymn was sung, and the benediction was given:

> Send us anywhere, O God, only go with us.
> Lay any burden upon us, only sustain us.
> Deprive us of anything, save thy Son, Jesus Christ.

It was an unusual benediction, and Jim was deep in prayer as it was spoken. I know because I peeked over at him, just at the moment I knew with absolute certainty that he would be entering the ministry. Of course he would be praying, if he had any inkling of what I had been made aware of! I wondered about his reticence to leave, for all five children were on a collision course with him as they made their hasty exit from the pew. Jim seemed strangely quiet and contemplative as we drove home.

At Sunday dinner, it was our custom to discuss the sermon we had just heard. Sometimes Jim would observe, "If I were a pastor, I would have said it like this ..." On this particular day, it was not lost on me that Jim's remark was, "*When* I'm a pastor, I would say it like ..." There was no guesswork involved about the subject to be discussed after dinner, when Jim asked to speak with me about something important.

God had heard the yearning of Jim's heart and, as any good father, delighted in giving his child that desire. Jim had been called.

It is one thing to receive a call on Sunday and quite another to wake up on Monday wondering—how would we support a family of seven, where would the money for tuition come from, how would our children respond to such a change of direction in their lives, and had we even heard correctly? God had been wonderfully good about letting us both know at the same moment, and considering that we had been a pew length apart, separated by our five children, we figured that we both could not have been mistaken. It was truly staggering in scope. Talk about shock and awe!

∽

A few miles from our home was the USA headquarters of WEC International, a mission organization that had 1,900 missionaries in countries all over the world. We had discovered the agency several months prior and had made friends with many missionaries on the home staff. We often availed ourselves of the monthly meetings and dinners that they held and, during one such evening a few weeks later, those in attendance were asked to share what God was doing in their lives. Jim rather cautiously shared his new call and, much to our amazement, those who knew us well responded that they had been aware for some time that we would be in full-time Christian service. They had been waiting for us to hear the Lord's call.

About the same time, while talking with a retired pastor whom we knew, I was interrupted by a question which seemed born out of frustration and impatience: "Lois, *when* are you and Jim going to serve the Lord full time?" It seemed as though everyone except us was aware of what God had planned for our lives. It was comforting, however, to know that our call had been perceived by so many others. That reinforcement would be even more valuable to us in the days to come, as we shared with those who meant most to us.

My mother, who had died some years before, would not have posed any opposition. In fact, we were sure that she was in the heavenly cheering squad and would have been one of our staunchest supporters. Dad, in his classic understated way, smiled, nodded his approval, and simply asked how we were going to manage the whole scenario.

It was the reaction of Mother and Dad Caldwell which surprised us. Quite disturbed at thinking we would not be able to support our family and Jim's engineering degree would be wasted, they asked for a special meeting with us. It was difficult to be regarded as deranged, irresponsible, and even arrogant in our determination to do what God had confirmed through so many others. We realized that there would be no support from that quarter. Eventually they did accept the fact that we were going to proceed, with or without their blessing, but there always remained skepticism that we would succeed.

We could somewhat understand their concerns, however, for we had some of the same doubts. Had it just been Jim and me, we might have made it "somehow." We never expected manna to fall from heaven, but we had no idea how this whole project was going to play out. For Jim to quit his job and enroll in seminary was more than even we could envision. God had gotten us into this and, as far as we could see, he was going to have a big job completing the task.

Still smarting, we went off to visit with our pastor. We were sure that he would understand, for we knew that one of his greatest desires was to see some in his flock seek seminary training for the pastorate. However, his idea of those qualified for such service was not those in their late thirties with five children, a mortgage, no savings account, and equipped with little else except a great deal of zeal and determination to go where they were being led. His response to our announcement was enough to pour water on any attempt. "Who do you think you are?" he asked. His wife followed with the observation, "You're not missionaries who someone will support. No one is going to hand you money." No one had to tell us that, for we knew no one who was even remotely a candidate for that role!

Looking back, it was quite clear that God had taken away all our supports, for he wanted us to be completely dependent on him. He would supply it all and would furnish the material for the pages of this tale himself. But at that point those pages were in the future, and it soon became crystal-clear that we were going to have to make choices that would entail leaving a great deal to follow him. I suspect that Jim read and reread the stories of Jesus asking the rich young ruler to go and sell all and the disciples having to choose between being obedient or remaining in their professions. Those stories in Scripture were certainly my constant reading material at the time.

The question was clear: would we love him more than people's approval, our security, the things we had acquired, and a safe existence for our family? It seemed that lessons in surrender were being met at every turn.

Collectibles were never high on our list of priorities, and we certainly never intended to have a collection. However, in our time overseas we had acquired a number of darling Hummel figurines. They had been inexpensive then, and I cherished them as memories of where we had been and delighted that I owned such nice and now valuable things. There were the five cute little orchestra men and one of a teacher with her little pupil, but my favorite was a triple figurine of a girl and her little brother, peering into a cradle at a newborn baby.

We had acquired the many utilitarian possessions that were necessary to support the rearing of five children, but my Hummels were some of the little niceties that took me into a special world of fancy and elegant things. They were carefully guarded and, of course, they were protected by house rules: no one was to touch them or lay anything next to them, and certainly no balls were to ever come into their presence—which was all well and good in theory, but not so adhered to in practice.

Jim's arms were full of a stack of hymnals as he entered the house one evening and, being in a hurry, he stacked them on the record player next to the orchestra people. The hymn book slide that followed was most remarkable. Jim, not one to be sloppy, had stacked the books with precision, tall and straight. I turned around just in time to see them tilt and fall, as if an invisible hand had carefully pushed them. The result was the shambles of three of the figurines and my equanimity.

Later, after a great deal of not-so-loving comment directed Jim's way, and some glue and skillful repair by him, the five little men sat playing their instruments again—but only for a short tour!

It was only a few days later that the boys were testing the properties of a newly-purchased soft cloth ball. They determined that, being soft, it didn't qualify as a truly legitimate ball, and tossing was not technically throwing. So with one swift toss, the two tiny men who had been untouched met their demise. Oh my! Could a mother be more upset? Out came the glue bottle again. Jim patiently fixed the Hummels, but nothing much was piecing back together my disgruntled soul.

Didn't God care about my things? Were all my lovely possessions to be taken away from me?

Actually, I was asking those questions the next week, as I was dusting the much-valued triple Hummel. As the dust cloth caught on the braid of the little figurine in my hand, it started on the same disastrous downward path. Resignedly, I let go completely and exclaimed to the Lord, "You can have them *all*, if you want them." I watched as the precious piece hit the floor and simply rolled across it, unscathed. No, God was not taking away all my lovely possessions. He was merely waiting for me to give them all into his care and keeping. As I finished my dusting, I pondered what other things I was clinging to so fiercely.

God was truly gracious to teach me with something so insignificant as china figurines for, in looking over my list of treasures, many were more valuable: my children, my marriage, my wonderful husband, my reputation, health, and a host of other things. It was not a matter of the Lord not wanting me to have them, but rather, would I give them to him and acknowledge that they had all had their origin in him? I recalled verses near the end of the well-known poem, "The Hound of Heaven," where God said to Francis Thompson,

> All which I took from thee, I did but take,
> Not for thy harms,
> But just that thou might'st seek it in my arms.

This was a matter of loving him more than these, of loving him more than our reputations and whether we were thought irresponsible, foolhardy, or stubborn, of loving him even more than our possessions and acquiring wealth. Would we trust him for everything, even our family's security?

A little-known book, *A Boy's War*, tells of Hudson Taylor III being interned in a concentration camp in China during World War II.[1] He was just a little boy at Cheefoo School, where missionary children attended as boarding students, when most of the country was overrun by the Japanese. His parents were in another part of China, and the book recounts the agony of his mother not knowing what would befall her son. Being totally incapable of doing anything, every day she released her son to the Lord with the faith that "if you take care of the things that are dear to God, He will take care of the things dear to you." Four years later, young Hudson was released unharmed, having continued his education under the instruction of their teachers, who had been interred with the children. Among those teachers was Eric Liddell, the Olympic gold-medal runner whose story was so well told in the movie *Chariots of Fire*.

It all began to make sense. It is well said that there is no place in which rests more security than in the Lord's will. We had given God all that we knew how, so he was now able to give it back to us in his timing, having been touched by his redemptive hand. It was not long until the returns started pouring in—but not before we got our feet wet by getting out of the boat.

CHAPTER 2

WALKING ON WATER

Jesus, Savior, pilot me
Over life's tempestuous sea;
Unknown waves before me roll,
Hiding rock and treacherous shoal;
Chart and compass come from Thee:
Jesus, Savior; pilot me.
>   —Edward Hopper

Then Peter got down out of the boat, walked on the water and came toward Jesus. But when he saw the wind, he was afraid and, beginning to sink, cried out, "Lord save me!" Immediately Jesus reached out his hand and caught him. "You of little faith," he said, "why did you doubt?"
>   —Matthew 14:29–31

AN INSIGHT INTO our spiritual nurture is that our church did not have a single Bible study at that time. Jim and I thought perhaps that would be a good place to begin, so I called the entire church roster. Less than a handful showed any interest: a teacher in the local school system, the student assistant pastor, and a high

13

school student, Jeff Okamoto. So with those few souls, we began to meet every other Friday evening to study God's Word.

During those months, we became quite friendly with Jeff and his brother, Wayne, and we invited them to dinner. It still mystifies me that people in their late thirties would hold any attraction for two high school students, but they accepted. It seemed a good time to tell them what our new path in life was going to be. So somewhere between chicken-and-dumplings and dessert, we shared with them that Jim was going to be leaving his job and starting seminary.

Being two very intelligent boys, they were quite aware of tuition costs and the size of the family with whom they were sharing dinner. They must have done some pretty quick calculations, and I can only attribute the silence that followed to their very polite natures and upbringing. Jim and I were becoming accustomed to extremes of reactions, so we waited for the usual "Are you kidding?" or "How can you possibly do that?" The truth was that we were dead serious and also didn't know how we would do it.

Expecting to have to try to explain that it was not something we had decided on a lark, and that God was going to have to both show us the blueprint and be the supply agent, we were surprised when Wayne gave us a big smile and said, "Wow! I always did want to see somebody walk on water!" He had captured it exactly. Jesus was calling, and all we had to do was to leave the boat and keep our eyes on him.

Wayne's little statement stuck with us throughout the following years. We would often think back to those words and be reminded that keeping our eyes on Jesus was the key to keeping us afloat. Jeff and Wayne could not have known how great their influence would be or how much of a boost it was to us, as they followed up with, "Hey, that's great! What's the plan? So when are you starting?"

We knew them well enough not to chalk up their reaction to teenage enthusiasm, but to recognize their sound conviction that what they were reading in the Bible was both true and of practical use for the present. They had a better understanding of God's trustworthiness than most adults we were encountering. They really believed that "Jesus Christ is the same yesterday and today and forever" (Heb. 13:8). If he could keep Peter afloat, he could keep us on top of it all.

The boys remained two of our biggest fans as we ran the course, and both are in Christian service today and remain our friends. Jeff, the elder of the two, is a Christian psychiatrist. In my lighter moments, I can't help wondering if seeing such a radical and improbable decision, made by two otherwise sane people, might have influenced his entry into that field!

The first wave we encountered came rushing at me as I looked at the budget book and did the math. This was no little wave; what I was looking at resembled a tidal wave! Seven people do not live on air, and the statement that people would not hand us money was resounding like a gong in my head.

One morning, Jim had left for the job he would soon be quitting; the children were off to the Christian school they attended, which cost us tuition we would not be able to afford; and the bills were staring at me. I was in no frame of mind to be teaching the Bible study I had begun with some women in the community, and I had a few minutes to be washed over with a wave of tears before the women would start arriving. Cry I did, and pleaded with the Lord to show us that he would provide.

It is not the best timing to be in the middle of a good cry when the doorbell rings. There was a hasty mop-up job. Not wanting to have to explain why their teacher was having such a difficult time trusting, I smiled and answered the door to find one of my neighbors arriving early.

Not even noticing my red eyes, she launched into a rather embarrassed explanation of why she had come earlier than everyone else. She was going to be moving (explanation of why and where), and she had stopped on the way to our house to close her bank accounts. In the process, she had discovered that the account they kept for tithe money had a small amount left in it. She informed me that, as it was tithe money and not her own, she felt the Lord would have her give it to me (long explanation of how she knew what the Lord had told her). With that, she thrust an envelope into my hand, in which I found ten dollars and eighty-seven cents. By then she was out of breath and I was just as speechless, but for a different reason.

Could there be a clearer illustration that perhaps people actually would hand us money—or would be used as God's instruments for giving it to us? It was not a lot of cash, and certainly would not buy much more than a gallon of milk and a few loaves of bread, but it was sufficient for us to begin to understand that God, indeed, would be the provider. It didn't matter what people said; what mattered was that God really did have the chart and compass.

Having fortified us with that assurance and object lesson, God next firmly let us know that we were to proceed with this whole adventure without accruing any debt. Jim told me that he had become aware that God did not want us to have any loans, credit-card debt, or financial obligations of any kind. Had I not just had a similar conversation with God, I would have been sure that Jim was being more literal than needed. After all, whoever heard of facing three years at Princeton Seminary without running up student loans? How about feeding seven of us and buying clothes for children, who thought nothing of growing two or more inches a year, not to mention paying off the car loan?

By this time, we had ceased being surprised when God upped the ante; we were just in a state of wondering. We wondered what was coming next, wondered how he would come through each time, and wondered if we could possibly do what was being asked of us. One thing we did *not* wonder about was that we were together in this, and we clung to each other. But really! Not even a loan to help us out?

We cashed in the little bit we had in a mutual fund. As it turned out, the stock was traded on the day it was the lowest in years, but we were able to pay off all of our debts except the car payment. With the little left over, we could purchase a color TV for the family. We knew that there would be no going to movies, and our old black and white TV was taking twenty minutes for the picture to appear, so a new TV seemed a wise investment.

There was just enough. Why, oh why was there never any extra? Why couldn't we have made a profit in the stock market like so many others we knew? And then there was the matter of that ongoing car payment.

Our income matched the outgo and nothing was ever left over, so it was apparent that we were not going to be able to pay off the car. I rationalized that perhaps one debt was not going to bother the Lord. I was right: it didn't bother him, because he had the answer.

A few nights later, I was talking on the phone with my brother when the subject of the car debt came up. Without hesitation, Bob offered to lend us the money to pay it off. I was delighted and rejoiced "with exceeding joy"—until it hit me that a loan from Bob was still a loan. I realized that I would have to call him back and refuse his more-than-generous offer. Oh, why was I always in these awkward positions?

With dread and hesitation, I called Bob back to explain the situation. What would this do to our relationship, how rigid would my explanation sound to him, and how ungrateful might he perceive me? Bob listened to my halting explanation, immediately understood, and with no hesitation offered to pay off the entire loan!

How could I think that God would not have a plan? It is one of life's greatest amazements that he does not shake his head and turn away, or chastise us in some fashion, when we do not trust. Instead, he makes us all the more aware of his great love and draws us even closer. What had seemed so awkward and impossible cemented an even greater bond of love between my brother and me—and was another step in our being drawn even closer to the heart of God.

◯

While I was riding the waves of financial improbabilities, Jim was applying to Princeton Seminary. While it is quite common today to have middle-aged people seek a second career in the ministry, it was new and not readily accepted then. There were those, Jim discovered, who actually questioned whether a man of his advanced years (all thirty-eight of them) could possibly be capable of learning Hebrew and Greek, let alone grapple with theological subjects. Princeton's response was that Jim could enter seminary on a part-time basis.

Well, that just wasn't going to work, and we didn't need God to tell us so. With five children, we could not be stringing this along for years. It was an all-or-nothing proposition. Just how would we go about telling the seminary that they hadn't got the message straight?

A trip to Princeton, to talk with Admissions and the person in charge of financial aid, seemed a good idea. After forty miles plus those visits, we were standing in yet another outer office, waiting to plead our case. The door opened and a distinguished gentleman entered, shaking rain from his umbrella. Having nearly run into us and given us a good sprinkling, he turned to apologize and asked if he could be of help. At that moment, anyone willing to be of aid was a welcome sight, wet or not! He ushered us into a large office, introduced himself, and asked our business.

We recounted our dilemma and waited while he pondered it. Our host commented that he was sure Jim had enough brain power to handle the courses and that he would arrange for full-time admission. By then, Jim had regained enough composure to wonder what position was held by this gentleman behind such a big desk and ventured to ask him. "Oh, I'm sorry. I should have told you; I'm Dean of the Seminary." It was instantly apparent that he most certainly could arrange things! Dean Adams holds a soft spot in our hearts to this day, wet umbrella and all.

Off we went to the financial aid office, after being assured that we would be well received. Now we were back to looking at finances, a dismal scene if there ever was one. We laid out all the figures and the vacuum of expected help from church, family, and friends. There was a quick response: "Hmmm. Your need is obvious."

I vacillated between wanting to ask what he was going to do about it, if anything, and wanting to deck the man. How dare he call me needy! I had never wanted for anything serious, my needs had always been met, and here was this man saying I was *needy*! I felt like some poverty-stricken child.

Jim acknowledged the aid officer's assessment to be accurate and didn't seem the least bothered by the pronouncement. That was enough to bring me down to reality. We *were* needy. We were financially needy, but more sobering, we would be the most barren of people without the Lord meeting *every* need we had. Our salvation had been provided by him, our sustenance had been his doing, and our every breath was his good gift to us. Perhaps being needy was not such a bad idea. Perhaps it was just another opportunity for God to supply.

With an inward apology to our interviewer and an even more sincere one to God, I straightened my wounded pride and waited with relish to see what would happen next. I was not to be disappointed, but then I never have been with God's doings. We were assured that, given our need, we would be receiving full financial aid: Jim's tuition would be paid! Now all we had to do was figure out how we would exist.

There was no question that I would have to return to teaching, but I shuddered to think of how far a teacher's pay would go in providing for the seven of us. The public school system seemed like a good place to start applying, because the pay there far exceeded the pay of a teacher in a Christian school.

When I went to apply at the public school, I was told that there was an abundance of teachers at the moment; they had received eight hundred applications for a handful of openings. Jim, however, seemed relieved; he kept saying that he was sure I was to teach where the children went to school, so our lives might not be too separate and our vacations would fall together.

Off I went to Phil-Mont Christian Academy, where our children attended, only to be told that there were no openings there, either. I returned to the car, put my head on the steering wheel, and prayed: "Dear Lord, you heard what I was just told. I can't ask for someone else's job" (although the thought had crossed my mind), "and I can't hope that someone gets sick and needs a replacement. Please, create me a job. There's nothing more I can do, nowhere else to turn, and we have to eat." I didn't even bother with an "Amen." Dejected, I started the engine and returned home.

I was getting more than anxious at this point, for it was now June, and Jim would have to quit his job at the end of August to begin seminary in September. There was not much time for creating, although I had to admit that God had managed to create the whole world in a few days. I was willing for anything, and when another Christian school in the area offered me a position, I thought the problem was solved. I had forgotten who held the compass. The position was for less salary and would mean a different schedule for me than our children had, but who was I to argue with a solution?

Every time I went to sign the contract, however, I had such a feeling of unease that I gave up and wrote their school board what was undoubtedly the most unusual letter they had ever received: I thanked them for their offer, declined it, and explained that I knew God wanted me to teach at Phil-Mont, where our children attended. They knew, and I knew they knew, that there were no openings at Phil-Mont. I was turning down a job for one that didn't exist! I could only imagine how relieved they felt that such an unstable person was not going to be teaching in their school!

Imagine my surprise to receive a phone call from them, saying how impressed they were that someone was convinced she had to be exactly where the Lord wanted her. Therefore, they not only would hold the job for me until I was offered the non-existent position I sought, but they would pray for a position for me there.

I was overwhelmed, but not as overwhelmed as a few days later, when the principal of Phil-Mont called and asked if I were still available. They had just *created* a new position!

Mandatory bussing to private and parochial schools was just beginning, and Phil-Mont was about to receive its first children to be bussed from the city of Philadelphia. My position would be to bring thirteen students of fifth grade age, who tested at grade levels ranging from two to four, up to grade level in one year. Never mind that I didn't think to question whether it could be done. The school had no available rooms, so my room would be created out of an existing hallway to a fire exit, between the office and the teacher's room. It didn't matter to me how my room would look; it could have been up in a tree house for all I cared. Creation was still on God's agenda, and I had a job! We were set for lift-off!

As excited as we were, we quickly realized that my teacher's pay would not cover all the bills, and we had not forgotten the strong conviction that we were not to acquire any debt. We most likely would need about three thousand dollars more per year, according to our figuring. I knew that Jim's military veteran's benefits, which would have been about that amount but had never been used, would expire three months before he would need them.

Somehow I could not bring myself to accept that Jim had missed receiving them by such a narrow margin, so I called our congressman to verify that our information was correct. To my amazement, I was told that there was currently a bill before Congress to extend those benefits for three more years. Praying for "those in authority" (1 Tim. 2:1–2) suddenly became more than a vague concept, and we started to pray fervently for Congress. They passed the bill, which not only extended the benefits, but increased them.

About that time, Jim came under the care of our presbytery. On a particularly hot June day, we traveled into Philadelphia for Jim to give his testimony and receive approval to be a candidate for the ministry. By this time, we were no longer hesitant to state that we were sure God would provide, and Jim said so quite clearly. He was approved and home we went, but only to gather up my father and drive back into the city. For Father's Day, we had promised to take him to see one of his favorite musicals, *Show Boat*.

We were in no financial position to be paying for tickets to the Academy of Music, but Dad had been ill, and we realized that this probably would be the last time we could take him on such an outing. We both were hot and tired, and Jim was complaining loudly about not even having time to change his shirt and sport coat.

For once, I was the one to realize that we should do what was right, not what would come naturally. With my reminder that we should give thanks in all things, off we went with Dad—to sit in those expensive seats on the ground floor, where he would not have to negotiate steps.

At intermission, Jim went to get a drink at the nearby water fountain, only to hear behind him a voice asking, "Pardon me, but weren't you at Presbytery this morning?" There stood its moderator, Rev. Dr. Aaron Gast, who had recognized Jim from the clothes he had not had time to change! Not only that, but had we been tucked away in the more affordable seats in the balcony, the meeting never would have occurred. They chatted for a moment.

After the show, our paths crossed as we were leaving. Dr. Gast mentioned that he had been impressed with our willingness to pursue what appeared an improbable path, given the size of our family. He ventured that his church had a fund to help seminarians and, while he was almost certain it had already been committed for the coming year, he would like our name and address and would see what could be done. Though there was no assurance of immediate help, just the thought lifted our hearts. Besides, who would ever have imagined that such a series of events could be so ingeniously orchestrated?

That was Tuesday. On Saturday, we received a letter from the church's business administrator that the trustees, at their Wednesday evening meeting, had voted to give Princeton Seminary a thousand dollars a year for Jim! Before I could do cartwheels, Jim reminded me that when churches gave money in ways such as this, it was generally applied to the scholarship aid which the seminary was already giving. That meant we would never see it, but it was nice to know that God took care of the seminary, too.

When we received a letter from Princeton Seminary shortly thereafter, we were not surprised that they had been notified of the gift. What did surprise us was to read that the church had carefully worded their letter to say that the money was to be used for our *expenses.* After taking out Jim's student fees, the seminary would be sending us a check for eighty-five dollars each month. Jim is the only seminarian we know who was paid by the seminary to attend!

We had done our best at calculating our need, but our heavenly Father knew the future and how much more really would be required. Jim decided it might be a wise move to see if the firm he worked for would keep him for two days a week. He had been able to arrange all his classes so that they fell within three days each week and, even though working two full days would mean a terribly heavy schedule, it seemed like a good solution toward meeting our expenses. We were not too hopeful that such a boon would be granted, as companies usually do not cater to the requests of those whom they know are quitting.

Armed with only a dire sense of need and more hope than I could have mustered, Jim asked for part-time hours. His boss listened to the request and, after a consultation with those in higher management, returned with the proposition that Jim could work the days he had requested—*plus* they would like him to work full-time in the summers during seminary! Jim was delighted. When his boss added that Jim's new pay rate would be ten percent higher than he was presently earning, "overwhelmed" was a gargantuan understatement!

Only God could have been the author of it all. We had no doubt about that. Jim's engineering thinking had long since kicked in, and he had come to the firm conviction that such a series of amazing circumstances was far, far beyond any mathematical probability. We had echoed what the psalmist had said: "I am poor and needy; may the Lord think of me" (Ps. 40:17). He had not only thought of us; he had charted our course, calmed the seas, reached out his hand to steady the boat as we gingerly stepped out—and had filled our nets beyond our wildest imaginings.

CHAPTER 3

MOMENT BY MOMENT

He giveth more grace when the burdens grow greater,
He sendeth more strength when the labors increase;
To added affliction He addeth His mercy,
To multiplied trials His multiplied peace.[1]
— Annie Johnson Flint

Let us not become weary in doing good, for at the proper time we will reap a harvest if we do not give up.

— Galatians 6:9

I HAD STEADFASTLY insisted that I would never resume my teaching career as long as there were children at home to be cared for. Having to work because of real financial need was one thing, but in my mind, rearing children was a career in itself. I wanted to be the one to oversee the growth of my children. After all, who could do it better? Now here I was with four-year-old Dave, and I was going back to teaching in order to support the family. I was not a happy camper.

Day care was out of the question. It would cost too much, and it was not the environment I envisioned for Dave's life. There were no relatives to help out, and no ready solutions were in the offing. Every time I looked at Dave or hugged him to me, my heart sank. Of course I prayed about it; actually, grousing to God about my dilemma would be the better description of the petitions I was sending heavenward. I truly believed that he had given Dave into my care and I had given Dave back into his keeping. Only now it seemed as though God wasn't aware that time was running out, and this child in his keeping was about to not be cared for properly.

Somewhere in the back of my mind, I recalled something which had caught my attention years before, in one of the many classics I had read. It had been in a collection of writings by François Fénelon, a seventeenth century archbishop of Cambrai, France. Though banished to his own diocese for the latter years of his life, he remained a spiritual advisor to myriads of souls. His advice seemed wise and timely in my situation: "A life of faith produces two things. First it enables us to see God in everything. Secondly, it holds the mind in a state of readiness for whatever may be His will."[2]

God was somewhere in this, and perhaps I was not looking for his will. It occurred to me that it was my own will I was bent upon and that this life of faith and I needed to be better acquainted. I stopped grousing and waited ... and waited ... and waited. Okay, so "faith is being sure of what we hope for and certain of what we do not see" (Heb. 11:1). I continued to wait, although a bit uneasily and with only some small hope that God really would come through.

Donna Berger was one of my Bible study women, whom I had come to know as a cheerful, trusting Christian and a true prayer warrior. To my surprise, she had come to me a year or so before because she had seen my prayers answered. Her Roman Catholic background had included mainly prescribed prayers, and I assured her that praying from her heart was both desirable and acceptable to the Lord. After watching me pray and then asking,

"Is that all there is to it?" she had set off on a life of prayer that far outstripped her teacher's.

Now, as she was leaving the morning's study, she asked how our preparation for seminary was coming along. I shared all the ways the Lord had provided and mentioned that I would be starting to teach soon and how miraculously the job had appeared. I purposely left out the part about wondering if God would supply the impending need for Dave's care.

I had no sooner finished sharing when Donna asked how Dave would be cared for—and offered to watch him during my hours at school. Quickly, I thanked her for the offer but reminded her that we had no money for child care, so it would be impossible to accept her kindness. Wreathed in smiles, she responded in her exuberant way, "Oh, I never said anything about money. I'd love to watch Dave. Don't worry about a thing! I'm just glad to be a part of it all!"

Fénelon was right: faith does enable us to see God in everything, and I saw his hand all over this arrangement. Certainly now I would be more willing and ready to do his will.

God had picked just the right person for the care of his child, far better than I could have found! Not only had Donna reared eight children of her own, and certainly was eminently qualified for the child care part, but she lived only two blocks from the school where I would be teaching! This meant that the children and I could all start our mornings together, and there would be no long treks to deliver Dave somewhere. I also felt that he would be more secure, knowing I was close by.

Actually, I doubt there was much thought of me at all during his busy days with Donna. Among all the things they did, every week he'd gather up a dandelion bouquet and accompany her in making visits to a nearby home for the elderly. Little did any of us realize that God had a plan in that too, for the far-reaching effects of those visits were to unfold many years later. Yes, Donna had been correct; I need not have worried.

So September arrived and the school year began. Peanut butter sandwiches were made and clothes were laid out the night before, lunches were packed, school books were gathered, breakfast was at the ready for the morning rush, showers were timed so that we could all arrive clean, the car was gassed and ready, and off we all went. We could not have looked more like a caravan on its way to market.

We arrived in good order. The children climbed out of the car, sorted out their belongings, and took off in the directions of their various classrooms. Squaring my shoulders, I reported for duty with the anticipation of seeing my newly created classroom and meeting my newly created class.

A swift inventory was in order. There they were, a class such as that school had never seen—nor I either, for that matter. Thirteen eager faces stared back at me for a moment, although eager for what, I wasn't sure. One returned to reading a comic book, two or three resumed milling around the room, one went back to sleep inside his turtleneck sweater, two looked ready to challenge any authority that might come their way, one girl was strutting her stuff, and a smaller girl appeared overwhelmed and confounded by the whole situation.

She wasn't the only one! I began to wonder whether the eager looks were not an unspoken laying down of the gauntlet, as to who would really be in charge.

I realized that most of these children had been bussed from Philadelphia and had not had the multitude of opportunities that our suburban children experienced. I was going to have to address more than their varied academic levels. Character, truthfulness, accepting authority, and respect—for God and me and each other—were all going to part of my curriculum for these students. In fact, to put it bluntly, civility was going to have to come before subject matter.

As for subject matter, it would be easier to start them on a second grade level together. To bring them up to be ready for sixth grade at the end of the year was not only improbable, it was inconceivable, it had to be impossible, it was an unheard-of situation, it was … it was the job God had given me to do.

In the fifteenth century, Brother Lawrence, a lay brother among the Carmelite monks in Paris, had written, "though it is difficult, we know also that we can do all things with the grace of God, which He never refuses to them who ask it earnestly."[3] As far as I knew, Brother Lawrence had only to face a mountain of pots and pans each day, not this class at which I was staring. However, if it was grace that would see me complete the task I had been handed, then grace I was going to ask for, and quite earnestly.

The days progressed, and the grace for which I had been pleading was poured out in great measure. I found myself creating interesting incentives for the children, ways to make literature and reading enjoyable, ideas for producing pride in themselves by performing for other classes, games to challenge them in math skills, and even different ways to learn the various Scripture passages that were required learning in the school. We sang them! We sang a least a hundred Scripture songs, until the office staff on the one side of our makeshift room and the occupants of the teachers' room on the other side must have wished for blessed silence.

Expectations for manners were set at the highest level: the students had been told, repeatedly, that there would be no field trips until I could be confident they would not disgrace the school or me, but would be such sterling examples of decorum that people would be in awe at their behavior. I figured it was safe to assume it would be a long time until we went on a field trip.

All this was done amid some very strange events. We started to keep a record of all the answers to the prayers during our devotional time each morning, prayers about situations for which I had never prayed before. There were petitions that there would be enough money for rent and that the landlord would not evict their family, that parents would stop fighting and not hurt each other or get divorced, that the neighbor's daughter who had been raped the night before would be okay, that the gangs would not hurt them when they got off the bus after school, and that they would be able to find a job before or after school to help the family finances.

My own silent prayer was that, before they left my class, each of them would come to know the Lord Jesus. Even though it was a requirement that at least one parent be a Christian to enroll a child in the school, only one student in the class believed that the Lord was real. Prayer time in the beginning seemed only an exercise to please me and get to go on that field trip they all wanted so badly.

It was the end of October when the subject of a field trip to William Penn's mansion was broached, but not before I had been to the dentist about my jaw, which was hurting most of the time. The malady, I was informed, was from clenching my teeth, something a field trip did not promise to alleviate. The rules were laid down: shirts were to be tucked in, girls would wear dresses, and boys would wear a shirt and tie. "Yes, ma'am," "thank you," "pardon me," and other of Emily Post's polite phrases would be part of their vocabulary, and the boys would see to the safety and needs of the girls and myself. It was a lot to ask.

The day arrived gray, with the promise of rain. Praying before we left, I hastily added, "and please, Lord, don't let it rain." Larry reminded me in no uncertain terms that if God wanted it to rain, then it was going to rain, and no amount of prayer was going to change the weather. I countered with a prayer that God would not want it to rain. Larry harrumphed his way into the cars with the other students, and off we went.

Noontime was our first real breakthrough. Lunch at McDonald's could have been a repast at the Ritz. The boys ordered for the girls, carried their trays, and paid. The girls were the picture of decorum and feminine grace, though a few snickers crept in. One by one the older patrons, who were watching all this, came and asked where these exemplary students were from and complimented them on their behavior. Chests puffed out, snickers stopped, and smiles broke out all over. They were so proud of themselves that they could have popped!

The afternoon progressed just a little ahead of the rain, and just as we were safely in the cars to return to the school, the first few raindrops appeared on the windshield. Larry had to admit that perhaps God had not wanted it to rain on our field trip and, just perhaps, prayer might work after all. Prayer now had meaning, and the fact that we could talk to God and he would hear and love us enough to answer was not lost on anyone, nor was the result of mannerly and polite behavior.

It was a long year, but grace won the day. We finished the year with eight pages of prayer requests which had all been answered, every student had come to know the Lord, the math achievement tests scored at tenth grade level, all would be promoted, my jaw had stopped hurting, and Larry would go on to express an interest in becoming a preacher.

Truly, with God all things *are* possible!

All things being possible, however, does not necessarily assure that all things are comfortable and without hardship. While all this was transpiring, Jim was jumping into the waters of Greek and Hebrew, theology, and homiletics. It was quite a shift, from the few thin engineering books which had kept him occupied for semesters, to the tomes of reading now to be digested. He quickly learned the value of drinking coffee and the necessity of finding some peace and quiet. Five children produce decibel levels not conducive to study, and their dad was too accessible for helping with science projects and repairing toys.

It was decided that Jim would spend two nights a week in Princeton, so he could work in the silence of the library and also cut down on gas consumption, for each round trip was eighty miles. Friends offered to let Jim sleep in their living room, a not-too-comfortable arrangement but at least a place to lay his head.

I, on the other hand, would have given anything for a full night's rest. Life was beginning to get to me. I was up at six every morning, taught a full day, and then returned home—to get dinner, help with homework, do the washing and ironing (yes, we ironed in those days!), finish my own paperwork, put the children to bed, and then often put in a few hours typing Jim's papers. Not that I had any typing skills, mind you. Jim typed by the hunt-and-peck method; it was just that I hunted and pecked faster than he did. How I hated those papers with Hebrew or Greek words! How many spaces should I leave for those crazy characters? The makers of that expensive erasable typing paper must have leapt for joy when they saw us coming.

The only redeeming value to it all was my own seminary education by osmosis, which was coming along quite nicely. Getting to bed at one or two in the morning to face waking up four hours later, however, did nothing to make me grateful for such a gift.

By November, I was so tired that I woke up crying every morning, not so much because I had yet another day to face, but because I hadn't died during the night and been relieved of it all. Jim, poor man, was on the horns of a dilemma: leave before I woke up and do what God was calling him to do, or stay and comfort me. The truth was that no amount of comfort was going to change the situation. I had thought God wouldn't allow more than a person could bear. Couldn't he see that I was folding?

It was just too much! One morning, as I was sitting on the edge of the bed, hesitating to put my feet firmly on the floor and start yet another day, I was aware of God speaking to me (however he does that thing with his still, small voice): "It will be three years, dear one, not one day less and not one day more. Will you do it your way or my way?"

Well, it wasn't working my way, so I gave up. Beside, he had called me "dear." He really did care about me; he did love me. "What's your way?" I asked. The answer was profound: "Go brush your teeth." I was too tired to argue about where this was going, so I compliantly went and brushed my teeth. "Get dressed." I got dressed. "Go wake the children." Off I went. "Get breakfast." I made breakfast. And so it went until later that morning. As I was giving my class a timed arithmetic test, I glanced up at the clock and realized the morning had flown by. I was not excruciatingly tired, and I had just had my first lesson in moment-by-moment living.

We are expected to think and plan for the future, of course, but not to let it overcome us. I could manage the moment, just not the whole day at once. It really was true: God gives just what we need, just when we need it and not before. I recalled Corrie ten Boom's father explaining to her that he gave her the train ticket just before getting on the train, not a day or a week ahead.[4] And I concluded that maybe Scarlet O'Hara wasn't all wrong when she met her obstacles by declaring she would think about them another day. The difference now was that I knew that God was thinking about my obstacles every moment. I just had to brush my teeth when he told me to!

As we approached Thanksgiving Day, I could say with Job, "Surely, O God, you have worn me out" (Job 16:7). I may have grasped the concept of living in the present and not borrowing trouble, but the thought of preparing a Thanksgiving feast for our family, plus my dad and Jim's parents, was enough to start tears flowing again.

After we realized that we would need more support and encouragement than our church was willing to provide, God led us to Narberth Presbyterian Church, where we were welcomed with love and open arms. Pastor George Callahan understood our call and included us in all the fellowship meetings right from the start.

So it seemed natural to share, at a prayer group there, that I didn't see how I could face the coming holiday. These were committed Christians and serious prayer partners, who were intent on helping each other live the Christian life, so I was unprepared to hear one of the women comment that perhaps I was feeling sorry for myself.

There undoubtedly was truth in that statement, for I certainly was feeling sorry that I had to face turkey and gravy and the trimmings that would be expected. But it sent me over the edge. I was going on fumes, something she knew nothing about in her sheltered life of having one child, money that seemed to bloom in profusion without her having to work for it, and a healthy father and mother who babysat and gave her days off for fun and games. What had happened to the scriptural injunction to "weep with those who weep" (Rom. 12:15, NASB)?

This was another step, learning that God's way means not to judge as she had, but rather to offer compassion. Even the Native Americans had understood not to think harshly until they had walked a mile in another's moccasins. It was one of those lessons that needed to be tucked away for future use. Years later, it would be used over and over again, when counselees would be coming for my help. How quickly we learn when we walk the path ourselves!

No sooner had we weathered Thanksgiving than we were faced with the Christmas holidays. We had always loved the season of Advent through New Year's Day. Unlike the magazines' allusion to a stress-filled time of year, it was our favorite season—filled with fun, laughter, and joy. But this year, just thinking about it all took more energy than I could conjure up, and I went limp at the mere thought of us looking for a tree and decorating.

It was just as well that I was too exhausted to go shopping for presents, because the budget was in no shape to even think about gifts. Jim and I wondered how we would tell the children that this would be the Christmas that wasn't. Of course there would be all the church-related activities, and Jesus' birth would still be the highlight, but we were going to seem like the Grinch who stole Christmas.

Jim was just as tired as I was. He was carrying a full load at seminary, traveling back and forth, working two days a week at his engineering job, playing mechanic to keep the cars running, and trying to stuff his head full of biblical Greek. And he knew that he needed to bring home good grades, because his report card would be at least as well examined by our children as theirs were by us. It was not unusual to see him pushing a grocery cart around the supermarket with his Greek cards in hand or waiting at the back of the church while we hung up our coats, mumbling words that only the biblical writers could understand.

Tangling with tree lights and cleaning up Christmas tree needles would be the straws that would break the camel's back. There would be no Christmas tree, and there would be no presents.

Now I knew the biblical saying, "as he thinketh in his heart, so is he" (Prov. 23:7, KJV). As hard as I tried to convince myself that this would be good for us all, and as cheerful as I tried to be about it, a joyous person did not emerge. What did emerge was another jewel from the writings of Fénelon: "I pray to Him not that He may take away your grief from you, but that He may make it a blessing to you; that He may give you strength to support it, and that He may not let you sink under it."[5]

Both Jim and I were having a hard time staying afloat. It was so hard to see any blessing in it that we gave up trying. That's what God was waiting for, so that he might work unhindered and all would be attributed to his grace and mercy. Whereas the logical approach is to put your shoulder to the wheel and try harder, surrender often wins the victory.

After we accepted that there would be neither tree nor presents, God took only until the following Sunday to pour out mercy. Pastor George asked to speak to us after church. He told us that it was quite apparent that we needed a break and offered us the use of his lovely Cape Cod home for Christmas week. Not wanting us to feel uncomfortable, as he knew we could not afford any rent, he informed us that he needed the pine needles cleared from the gutters. Could we do that?

It is amazing how the sinking ship started to float again at the prospect of a lovely New England Christmas around a warm fire. We wouldn't need a tree after all, for the woods surrounding the house smelled of pine, and the myriad of stars would be better than any Christmas tree lights. Being outdoors and clearing pine needles for a few hours would only add to the fun. The children could hardly wait to go!

∾

The blessings went to overflowing. Every year, Princeton Seminary gave prizes to all those who could pass a test for memorizing the Westminster Shorter Catechism. Jim decided to try his hand at winning, so he made an audio tape of the catechism and listened to it over and over again on those long drives, back and forth to seminary. It was a good deterrent against slumber, although as the weeks wore on he most likely could have recited the whole thing in his sleep! The exam was two weeks before Christmas. Just before the holiday break, a letter in his mailbox announced that he had indeed won the prize of $150!

Then, just for good measure, God graced us with another lovely gift. Never before, in the history of the school where I taught, had a bonus been given to the teachers. As a private school, our salaries were difficult enough to meet. This particular year, however, a generous gift had been given to the school for the purpose of giving every teacher a Christmas bonus, so accompanying our last paycheck of the year was an additional check, for $250!

$150 plus $250 equals $400 so, even after a tithe of forty dollars, we were $360 richer. Some hurried Christmas present shopping was done, gas to Cape Cod was paid for and, like Tiny Tim, we knew that God had blessed us, every one!

Yes, God had sent his Son, the greatest gift of all, but he was also in the business of giving multiple other gifts. It was just that *he* wanted to be the giver, and being compassionate, he didn't want us to shoulder the burden of trying to provide them.

This part of the story would not be complete, however, without a lesson in God's arithmetic and in how he uses events to shape our lives. Just before all this was transpiring, we were attending a mid-week church service and heard the plea of a local Japanese pastor for money for his struggling congregation. Jim and I carefully kept our tithe money in a separate account, for we knew how tempting it would be to use it for expenses when finances were strained.

Jim asked how much we had in the tithe account. We had only forty dollars. Nevertheless, Jim suggested we give the entire amount, rationalizing that it was not our money anyhow.

I often looked at the tithe account as insurance, should a medical bill stare us in the face. It was revealing to see how dependent we were on the checkbook balance and how easily temptation could enter. I wrote the forty dollar check for the Japanese church and sighed a little as the plate was passed and I dropped it in. There was now no money, God's or ours, to fall back on.

It was only a week or so later that the prize money and the bonus were ours, and the forty dollars tithe on them had replenished that account. Don't ever let anyone tell you that God doesn't do math! Also, that set of circumstances had revealed not only our weakness but the fruits of obedience. As the writer of a hymn said,

> Trusting in our Father's wise bestowment,
> I've no cause for worry or for fear.
> —Lina Sandell-Berg, "Day by Day"

The remainder of that school year went much more smoothly. Nothing diminished the work load, and our shoulders sagged from time to time, but now that our hope was more firmly rooted in the Lord, we found that our strength really was renewed. Our hearts could soar like eagles, we could run and not be weary, and we could walk on through the wind and storms and not faint. Walking moment-by-moment had reaped a harvest of peace, and being tired beyond our own strength had indeed been a blessing in disguise.

> His love has no limit, His grace has no measure,
> His pow'r has no boundary known unto men;
> For out of His infinite riches in Jesus
> He giveth and giveth and giveth again![6]
> —Annie Johnson Flint

CHAPTER 4

BICYCLES, BUCKETS OF PLUMS, ANGELS WITH IRONING BOARDS, AND SONIC BOOMS

Every joy or trial falleth from above,
Traced upon our dial by the Sun of Love.
We may trust Him fully, all for us to do;
Those who trust Him wholly find Him wholly true.
> —Frances R. Havergal,
> "Like a River Glorious"

When times are good, be happy;
but when times are bad, consider:
God has made the one as well as the other.
> —Ecclesiastes 7:14

Command those ... to put their hope in God,
who richly provides us with everything for our
enjoyment.
> —1 Timothy 6:17

SADLY, A GREAT many Christians have no distinct experiences of the greatness and scope of the heart of God. That heart definitely is where following Jesus will take us, where he longs to have us dwell. We know that now, but when we began we were only dimly aware of what following Jesus might mean, and I suppose we were not much different from others in our understanding. We had been what one might describe as a very ordinary family—that is, until God started to do extraordinary things. These events didn't elevate us above others, but they did elevate our vision and let us peer into the depths of God's goodness and faithfulness.

∽

In the backyard of our home was what we referred to as "our little orchard." The previous owners had planted nearly a dozen dwarf fruit trees, and they had lived on the premises long enough to establish the trees but had never seen the fruit (literally) of their labors. We were reaping what they had sown.

From June through October, we had a succession of cherries, apricots, peaches, plums, pears, and three kinds of apples. We sprayed, thinned, picked, cooked, and kept ourselves supplied all year with fresh-baked and frozen pies, cobblers, dumplings, butters, and sauces. The freezer shelves were stacked with these goodies. This ensured that the children had their supply of vitamins throughout the winter months, and the food budget was considerably reduced.

Not being farmers at heart, it was a few years before we discovered the secrets of good fruit production, the main one being the proper pruning of the trees in early spring. There was only one drawback. We realized that we could not properly do the pruning ourselves; an experienced tree service was required. I shall never forget the first year it was done; it seemed that the poor trees had been hacked to a sure state of non-survival, only to surprise us with bigger and better fruit.

When I looked more closely at the fifteenth chapter of John, it dawned on me how pruning was producing a better crop. It was a vivid object lesson in pruning and fruitfulness in our own lives, as Christians.

We made it a habit to budget for the pruning and found a reliable and very accomplished nurseryman, who did the work before the sap began to flow. For several years preceding the seminary era, he faithfully pruned and readied the trees for their bearing season, and it usually cost us about $200 for his services. Given our present budget, we would have to forego the pruning and hence the wonderful harvest of fruit, unless I could save enough to have it done. After managing to squeeze out some money, although not nearly the entire amount, I decided to call our nurseryman and have just a fraction of the work done.

Upon his arrival, I instructed him to do what he could for seventy dollars. Lest he think I was not aware of what that meant, I explained that Jim was presently not employed and that we would be in these straits for the next two years as well, while he attended seminary. Our nurseryman nodded and went off to the backyard with pruning shears in hand.

As it was a cold day and I had much to do around the house, I never once checked to see what he was doing and lost all track of time. A few hours later, he knocked on the door and asked me to check his work. As I rounded the side of the house and saw the trees, my heart sank. He had pruned all of them, just as he always had! Had he not understood? Had I not made myself clear? Would we have to eat beans so we could pay the bill? My look of horror produced a smile but no explanation.

"Didn't you understand? I asked you to do only seventy dollars worth," I gulped. Without even blinking, he replied, "This *is* seventy dollars worth."

Then he went on to explain that, as a young man, he had felt the Lord calling him to be a minister. As he put it, the things of the world had taken precedence and he had never pursued that vocation. Even though he had married instead, God had taken care of him and his family all these years, and he had experienced God's love in a deep and abiding way. "So," he announced, "now I have an opportunity to help someone else do what I did not. I will prune your trees as long as your husband is studying to serve God." The tears in my eyes were dangerously close to freezing in the cold wind, but the wind of the Spirit was warm as it blew around two of God's children that day.

In the back corner of the yard that spring, the well-pruned plum tree blossomed with small white flowers, and soon the fruit started to make its appearance. There was such profusion that the fruit looked like clusters of grapes, and the branches were groaning with the weight.

To assure full size and mature fruit, a large amount of the new fruit must be stripped away, which seems like a terrible waste but is necessary for a good crop. We stripped, and the large, golden Green Gage plums that resulted were so abundant that we offered them to everyone in the neighborhood who would come and pick them. We ate plums in every conceivable form and made jars of plum butter. We were plumb worn out with plums!

Nearby was WEC's USA mission headquarters. We knew their staff and candidates would appreciate some fresh fruit, so we urged them to come and take as much as they could. After picking industriously, home they went with two full bushel baskets of plums. Finally, we could stop eating plums.

A few nights later, we joined them at WEC for their monthly dinner, which was open to the public. After a plain but enjoyable meal, peppered with good fellowship and conversation, it was announced that there was a real treat in store for dessert. We watched with anticipation for this wonderful delicacy to appear, and so it did: a bowl of our Green Gage plums on every table! I prefer to think of this as a lesson in bread cast upon the waters returning, rather than the overflow of quail which the Israelites experienced when they complained about their steady diet of manna.

Pruning and plums were not the only things which the Lord provided. His vast range of capabilities was only beginning to make itself known. I knew that looking after the sparrows was on his list, but never did I dream that bicycles or filing cabinets would make the lineup.

We were approaching the first summer since Jim had entered seminary, and it promised to be a long one with five children and only one bicycle. Why I thought Jim could solve the problem I didn't know, but I did ask him. He confirmed my belief that there was no money hiding under the mattress and that one bicycle was all there was going to be. When I asked what I should do, his answer was straight and to the point: pray about it.

Wishing he had been more creative, I turned to leave the room and had just about made it to the door when he added, "And while you're at it, will you pray for a filing cabinet for me? I'm getting inundated with papers and I need some storage other than boxes." Good grief! Did the man actually think bicycles and filing cabinets dropped from heaven?

Thinking about it, I figured the bike was a lost cause. However, maybe I could scare up enough money for one of those used filing cabinets which could often be found at business auctions held in our area. Vacation Bible School was beginning and, as I entered the church, I stopped in the office to see if any notices had been posted about an upcoming sale. Seeing none, I asked the secretary if she knew of any. She replied that there had not been any for some time. Then without a pause, I heard from a woman standing behind me, "If you needed a bicycle, I could supply one."

Admittedly, I thought my hearing needed checking, but this benefactress assured me that she was in the midst of cleaning her garage and wished to divest herself of a bike that was taking up space there. A quick trip to her home after VBS netted me an almost new Schwinn bicycle! I loaded the bike into the back of our station wagon and rode home on cloud nine. I could hardly wait to tell Jim!

Guests were coming for dinner that evening, so I decided to keep the astounding news to myself until we said grace. Then I would thank the Lord and watch the expression on Jim's face. I almost made it, but just as we were all sitting down, I burst out with "You'll never guess what happened to me today. I got a bike!"

Before Jim could ask how, or I could register his expression, our guest looked up and said, "Too bad you didn't need a filing cabinet. I have an extra one of those." Forget my checking to see what expression was on Jim's face. God undoubtedly was checking out *my* expression!

Things like that don't just happen! You can put all the circumstances in the world together, and the probability still would be infinitesimal that bicycles and filing cabinets can appear "out of thin air" just when needed. Five children divided by two bicycles is a lot better than by one, and the summer was much more peaceful as a result. Jim's seminary papers found their resting place in the used gray filing cabinet, to be displaced by his sermons in the years that followed. Those two items were part of our household for a decade or more, reminders of what God can do.

Civilla D. Martin wrote the words of a well known hymn, "God Will Take Care of You," which captures the essence of the whole experience:

> All you may need He will provide,
> God will take care of you;
> Nothing you ask will be denied,
> God will take care of you.

A few experiences like ours give those words a ring of truth, especially if you are the ones riding the bike or filing your sermon notes. When people occasionally ask, "What is God like?" it is our delight to tell them this story, which could not better illustrate the care of God who loves so completely and provides so exactly.

Watching how God provided almost became Caldwell family entertainment. We never knew what to expect or how he would perform next, and quite often he did things when we were not even looking for an answer or solution. He simply knew what was needed. It was apparent that he could and would supply in the most unusual ways.

"We'd rather pray than pay," a motto we acquired, came about because of a few amazing answers to prayers for healing. When

Sue was six years old, she contracted viral pneumonia and was one very sick little girl. Coughing shook her frame from head to toe. The doctor told us that, unlike bacterial pneumonia, which can be helped with antibiotics, not much could be done until the disease ran its course.

Sue's temperature soared, her coughing was so severe that she was breaking blood vessels in her throat, and she alternated between chills and resembling a blast furnace. Before the weekend, the doctor advised us that, if she did not improve by Monday, a stay in the hospital with oxygen would be necessary. Saturday came and went with coughs getting louder, her temperature approaching the 105 degree mark, and Sue getting weaker.

Our home was a multilevel house, and Sue and Nancy slept on the top floor. The rest of the family's bedrooms were on the middle level, so I made Sue as comfortable as I could and went downstairs to my bedroom. I would try to catch a few winks before being awakened by those wracking coughs.

I woke about two in the morning and went upstairs. As I stood by her bed, I realized she was so hot that, without even touching her, I could feel heat radiating from her body. A mother does not do well when her child is burning up from within and she feels helpless to put out the fire. I was desperate. What could help?

Putting my hand on her head to see just how hot she was, I prayed. Actually, the prayer was more a statement than a plea: "Lord, if you were in this room, Sue would be well. I know I can't make a difference here, so I'll leave and you come to her." I did just that: I left. Full of fear, mind you, but I left. Somehow, in all my worry, I fell asleep.

I woke several hours later and immediately realized I had not been wakened by Sue's coughing! Never had a mother raced up stairs faster than I did, afraid that our daughter had died during the night while I had been sleeping. Feeling dismally irresponsible for having gone to sleep, and forgetting completely about my conversation with Jesus, I skidded to a stop by her bedside, only to realize that Sue's fever had broken and she was sleeping peacefully. I had slept soundly because there had been no coughing to wake me up!

Sue woke up full of pep and ready to go. And go we did—back to the doctor's office. Before she resumed climbing trees and chasing her brother around, I wanted to know that she really was well. The doctor checked her, compared the x-rays he had just taken with the ones that had been taken before, listened to her lungs, and then listened again. With a shake of his head he asked, "What happened? Sue not only is healed; she shows no signs of having had pneumonia."

On the way home, in the quiet of the car, I remembered Jairus's words to Jesus: "My little daughter is dying. Please come and put your hands on her so that she will be healed and live" (Mark 5:23). Jesus had, and she was healed.

Sue must have been pondering what had happened for, a year or so later, after her earache was healed when we prayed, she sat deep in thought for a while and then exclaimed, "Mommy! Jesus made a blind man see and a lame man walk. And Mommy, he healed *me*!" From then on, Sue's faith that Jesus can heal has never faltered. There is not a moment's doubt that dogs, cats, birds, and any other living thing can be healed by the Lord's touch.

So with twinkles in our eyes and smiles on our lips, but with great appreciation for the medical profession as well, our "We'd rather pray than pay" motto came into being. Certainly Jesus uses doctors to heal our ailments, but even if they can't, they can confirm what wondrous things our Jesus can do.

A few summers later, as we were preparing for another stress-free vacation in our pastor's home on Cape Cod, we were busily packing for the seven of us. This always took on the appearance of an army getting ready to move and required everyone's cooperation. The children and I were upstairs filling suitcases, and Jim was in the basement preparing boxes for all the food we'd be loading into our car-top carrier.

Suddenly the busyness was shattered by a yell from Jim that spelled only danger or disaster. We all ran to the basement to find

Jim standing in a pool of blood and the walls spattered with red.
He was holding his leg, which he had sliced while cutting a box.

We all went into action. I ran for a bandage to help stop the flow
of blood. Then, practically running the children over as I raced for
the phone, I shouted for them to pray as I dialed for the paramedics.
A friend went with Jim to the hospital while the children and I
paced the living room and asked Jesus for another touch, for Jim.

By the time Jim arrived at the emergency room, the bleeding
had stopped and the doctor was about to sew it up and send him
on his way. Just as he touched the cut, the geyser started spouting
all over again! There had been no loss of blood on the way to the
hospital, but the new bleeding prevented the wound from being
prematurely sewed and the artery then hemorrhaging inside. Jim
arrived home well-bandaged, and we departed only a little later
than we had planned.

Somehow, Jim managed to swim with a plastic bag around
his leg and sail his beloved sailboat with hardly any difficulty. As
far as the children were concerned, the doctors knew how to sew
well enough, but Jesus, who knows the workings of the body he
created, knew when to stop and start the blood flowing.

These little episodes resulted in our family's first line of
defense being prayer in any emergency. Even to this day, goldfish
and doggie ailments, science projects, exams, and aches or pains
get treated with prayer before calling in the regulars. Not that all
things get healed according to our wishes, but there is always the
great assurance that whatever happens, good or bad, we can trust
God with the outcome.

My father had finally reached that frustrating point of not being
able to drive. He no longer could shop for himself, his legs were
not dependable enough to climb into the bathtub to take showers,
and cooking healthy meals had lost its appeal for him. Taking him
into our home was not an option because of the stairs, and assisted
living had not yet made its appearance as an alternative.

There was only one thing to do: add his care to our already burgeoning schedule. This addition meant shopping for his food, preparing dinners several times per week, cleaning his apartment, and Jim bathing him.

Dad had a wonderful sense of humor and was always full of interesting tales and facts, which made the whole experience mostly pleasant for the children. It was also a great opportunity for getting help with homework.

While tiring and time-consuming, the whole scenario was not without its humorous moments, like the time Dad slipped off his bathtub seat while Jim was helping him bathe. Dad was thoroughly soaped, so the result was similar to trying to lift a greased pig. For a while, it looked like Dad might have soap suds for dinner that evening or the fire department would have to come to our rescue. Yes, there was laughter, and a merry heart did us all good, but the schedule was backbreaking, and concern over what the future held for Dad was constant.

Looking back, it is amazing what transpired during those long evenings. The children not only grew in respect and love for their grandfather, but they also gleaned much knowledge about aging and caring for others. In Dad, they always had a wonderful example before them of perseverance and a non-complaining spirit in the face of discomfort and limited abilities.

Not only that, but they all pitched in to clean his apartment, and Dad was a stickler for being neat and clean. His propensity for using lemon oil for dusting his furniture required our children to follow suit. They did so without complaint, although to this day they all shudder at the thought of oily, lemon-scented furniture polish. They also learned to do a good job with a cheerful countenance, which translated to their relationships with others, God, and their future employers.

At this point in relating our journey, it is appropriate to give space to our children and the way they managed through all our tight schedules, the change in direction of their lives, and all they were called upon to do. No child delights in shouldering more work when play is calling, and ours had not yet spouted halos. There were the normal expressions of "Do I have to?" and "Oh, no. Not *that*, too!" However, I would be hard put to find more involved and willing souls, for they cleaned every week—not just their rooms, but the entire house.

Sue could scrub a bathroom clean enough to eat off the floor, Nancy hung out in the kitchen and helped with the meals, and Bill's room was so neat it was almost incomprehensible that a teenage boy lived there. Kathy wielded a mean dust cloth, although that particular chore was far from her favorite. Dave, small as he was, toted trash and pushed the vacuum cleaner, which was shorter than he was if he stretched. As long as I live, one of my most precious memories will be of them bustling around the house, doing all that needed to be done.

As seminary progressed, Jim took on a student assistant pastor position, which required that he preach occasionally. Whenever that happened, the children would gather in a quiet place and pray for him to do well. Of course, the mere thought of their dad preaching and using them as examples in his sermons could have triggered fright, but watching their bowed heads and hearing their heartfelt petitions showed how much they truly cared.

The psalmist put it well: "Sons are a heritage from the Lord, children a reward from Him ... Blessed is the man whose quiver is full of them" (Ps. 127:3, 5). God had richly rewarded us with five, a full quiver (though sometimes, having our *hands* so full impressed us more).

Jim was well aware of the difficulties of my trying to juggle the roles of mother, wife, daughter, housekeeper, teacher, typist, and cheerleader for the family. He could see the cheerleading part was beginning to sag, and he inquired what he could do to make the load a little lighter for me.

Assessing the situation, I determined that it was the ironing that was threatening to sink my ship. After standing all day to teach, I trembled at the sight of ironing stacked like Mount Everest, but I could no more see Jim adding ironing to his own load than I could imagine him trying to run a mile in one minute. I figured I'd be doing the ironing until the rapture occurred.

My second year of teaching was beginning, and anyone who has ever taught knows the workload of preparing materials for a new school year, creating bulletin boards, and getting the classroom ready. It was more than enough, added to my family responsibilities, and I really thought I couldn't handle another thing. God thought otherwise.

One of my bridesmaids had married a doctor, and they were serving as missionaries in Nepal. The Hardings and their four children unexpectedly had to move up-country to Tansen, and Sue found herself having to teach her children where there was neither a school nor much in the way of books or supplies. Dick was busy with clinics in out-of-the-way mountain villages, and Sue needed all the help she could get.

The day before my school year began, I received a letter from Sue, asking whether it would be possible for me to gather the school books she needed and ship them to her. I couldn't imagine doing one more thing, and "not now" sounded like an appropriate response. I figured that obliging her would have to wait a few weeks (or maybe an eon or two).

The next day, as I passed out books to my own class, with every book I gave out came the inner question, "What about Sue?" Guilt never did sit well with me. I gave up. After school, I gathered up all the requested textbooks.

Sue's mother's house was nearby, so I decided to take the books there and ask if she would box and ship them. Mrs. Pierce assured me that they would be sent off to Sue within a day or two and profusely thanked me for all of my time and effort, especially when I was so busy with all I had to do. I carefully avoided telling her about my initial reaction.

Just as I was leaving the house, she hugged me and shared that she was in the sad position of being thousands of miles from her daughter and unable to do much for her. She went on to share that she had been praying about something she could do for someone else instead, and she felt that perhaps she could do something for me. Could she do my ironing? *Could she do my ironing?*

Now I know there are times when we entertain angels unaware, but I had known Mrs. Pierce half of my life and had never noticed her wearing wings. It didn't take me long to hug her and arrange to have the ironing sitting on our porch, where she would pick it up every Tuesday and return it by Friday.

We had many dinners together on those Friday evenings, when she returned our clothes freshly pressed and with buttons and tears repaired. During the two remaining school years we looked starched and ironed, and Mount Everest remained a mountain in Nepal instead of dwelling in my ironing basket.

Mrs. Pierce remained a close friend for years to come, and our children thought of her as a second grandmother and the savior of their mother's sanity. I thought of her as an exceptional and loving woman, a servant who would listen for the voice of the Lord and willingly obey.

I still marvel at how God arranges such things and lets people know what is needed, even when no request has been uttered. It remains one of the most glorious truths that God does all these things not just for our benefit, but for our enjoyment as well. Equally important is the awareness of how very much he cares. A few anonymously written lines so well define the thought:

> The thought, great wonder that it brings:
> My cares are all such little things,
> But to this truth I'll gladly cling,
> He cares for me.

51

As far as I know, there is nothing in Scripture to cover a sonic boom, as we called the mishap that occurred with our trusty brown Dodge station wagon. We had reached the point of needing two cars, since Jim and I were going in opposite directions each morning. The car that took us to school every day seemed entirely trustworthy and dependable. "Some trust in chariots and some in horses" (Ps. 20:7), but we trusted in our faithful Dodge to get us there and back.

On this particular morning, we were going through our normal routine of breakfast, gathering all the lunches for school, sorting out whose book bag belonged to whom, washing dishes, and trying not to trip over each other as we departed. We were running late, and the later it became the more our efforts were beginning to resemble a five-ring circus. I reached the point of no return and announced over the din, "Get to the car! And I don't want to hear a peep from any of you. *Not one!*"

Silence reigned as everyone filed out, got in the car, and quietly waited for me to start the engine and be on our way. Grim-faced, I turned the key, which immediately produced an explosion that rattled the windows of every house on the street. The hood of the car flew up, and pieces flew in every direction. Never had there been such a response to any action of mine! I sat stupefied. Doors could be heard slamming all over the neighborhood, as people flew out of their houses. From the back seat I heard, in hushed undertones, "Do you think we should tell her that the car just blew up?"

Not knowing what more to expect, I hustled everybody out of the car. From a respectful distance, we determined that Mount Vesuvius was not going to spew any more bolts, so I shut the hood. After ascertaining that there was no further danger, we accepted a neighbor's offer to take us all to school. I still had the teaching day in front of me and the awkward job of calling Jim, who was away at seminary, to explain that our car had just blown its cork. "What do you mean 'blew up'?" he asked. I meant just what I had said, but I figured he would have to see it to believe it. I heaved a sigh and determined that chariots of any kind do not deserve one's trust.

Jim figured he'd better make an appearance quickly and returned home that evening, to what appeared to be a normal vehicle. When he was about to think us all exaggerators of the greatest kind, he spied the broken hardware all over the driveway. It seems that gasoline had leaked from the carburetor into the crankcase, resulting in the explosion that would be the talk of the neighborhood for weeks to come. That there hadn't been more damage or that we had not been injured was truly God's hand.

That psalm about chariots begins, "May the LORD answer you when you are in distress; may the name of the God of Jacob protect you" (Ps. 20:1). Now we had all seen that "the LORD saves his anointed" (Ps. 20:6), and we were even more certain that trusting the Lord rather than chariots was the better way to go!

There is increasing tendency today for people to satisfy their own desires and to make their own way. Both of these approaches fall utterly short as means to experience God in ways that will let us know him and enjoy him forever. Abraham started a journey that fills books with its import, and he did it with only a few words from the Lord, which promised a destiny.

How much more did we have, as we were making our way on the path designed for us! We knew that God cared, would supply our needs, would protect us, would send people to help us when our knees buckled, would prune us so we would be more fruitful, and would "do immeasurably more than all we ask or imagine" (Eph. 3:20). We knew more than we had even dreamed possible about God's loving heart, which was exactly where we were heading as we kept following Jesus.

CHAPTER 5

WHALE SPOUTS AND SHOOTING STARS

Jesus, I am resting, resting
In the joy of what Thou art;
I am finding out the greatness
Of Thy loving heart.
—Jean Sophia Pigott

The LORD replied, "My Presence will go with you, and I will give you rest."
—Exodus 33:14

He makes me lie down in green pastures, he leads me beside quiet waters, he restores my soul.
—Psalm 23:2–3

A S WE SAW it, God used our summers for getting us caught up on household and family needs and for catching our breath. There was the fruit from our little orchard to deal with, but baking pies did not require marking papers or grading exams. Jim could return to his job and a more normal schedule, and we could all look forward to the vacation on Cape Cod, at the house that George and Bonnie Callahan reserved for our use two weeks each summer. However, God had better things in mind than just giving us a respite from work.

There is always danger, when one is serving the Lord, of concentrating so much on serving him that worshipping him and having fellowship with him take second place. Quite frankly, my prayer life had often degenerated to mostly bullet prayers, fired off like SOS flares, calling for help to get through the day. Likewise, it is easy for Bible reading to be displaced by theology books when they are the focus of seminary exams. There had been precious little time to dwell on the greatness of the God who was so lovingly supplying all our needs.

Over the years, I have come to the conclusion that God finds many more people willing to serve him than wanting to plumb the depths of his heart. Yet God's primary purpose for us in this whole venture was not to become informed *about* him, but to have fellowship *with* him. At that point, we were only beginning to be gripped by the depth of that truth. Our summers became a pleasant time for God to teach us, and Cape Cod became his classroom.

A flurry of preparations always preceded the long drive to New England. We made a routine of beginning our journey in the middle of the night, so our children would sleep through most of the drive. As we traveled, quiet reigned. I knew where everybody was, so I relaxed. Jim and I could listen to soft music, catch up on our own relationship, or just relish the peace. We would watch the dawn come up before waking everybody for breakfast, and then came the anticipation of almost being there.

Once we crossed the Sagamore Bridge, the world seemed to fall away behind us; we were on the Cape! We could smell the salt air, see the sailboats in the canal, and start counting the exits until we would reach Orleans and the summer mansion the Lord had provided for us.

Situated on a hill overlooking Crystal Lake, the house was surrounded by pine trees. The crunch of their needles underfoot always resulted in a woodsy pine scent in the air. It was not hard to see why the lake had acquired its name, for, as the sun glinted off the water, it sparkled and shimmered like crystals. The breeze, which would fill the sail of the little boat left for our use, played across the surface, and the water lapped against the sand of the small private beach in a mesmerizing pattern. In the early morning, a bob-white could often be heard announcing himself, and in the evening the crickets would sing us to sleep amidst the sounds of whatever animal was out among the pines, getting a last sip of water before he bedded down.

The house was truly lovely, with a big deck for looking down to the lake, a game room for the children, and decor that would do well in *House Beautiful* magazine. Oriental rugs graced the floors and there was a huge living room, the focal point of which was a cross of welded anchor chain over the fireplace. It would have been more than enough to be surrounded by the beauty outside, but to also live in it was a gift of pure pleasure.

Jim was excused from some of the settling-in process to check out the sailboat, which was his greatest delight. Now this boat, so dear to Jim, was nothing that would win the America's Cup. The little yellow Sunflower could hold only two people, but it could not have been sailed with more appreciation and care. It may have resembled a shallow yellow bathtub, but it was where Jim found a retreat from all the cares, studies, and worries of life. The children, Kathy in particular, enjoyed the times of sailing with their dad and each other.

As I prepared dinner, I often watched the children playing on the beach or in the water and Jim tacking back and forth, up and down the lake. A more idyllic setting we could not imagine, but God did not have in mind that we would just appreciate the beauty of our surroundings. It was to himself that he wished to draw us closer.

Rest, while necessary for the physical body, is likewise needed by the soul. The first did not elude us, for we never slept more soundly than in the quiet of those nights. With the press of activities at a minimum, our bodies were truly renewed. But it was meeting with God and seeing him in so many of our surroundings that produced such a bounty for our souls.

Sometimes, early in the morning before the children woke, Jim and I slipped out of the house with our Bibles and drove to the ocean. The sand dunes stood like barriers to protect us from the world, and we read or walked hand-in-hand, with no one around except God and a few busy seagulls.

On such a morning, while Jim had walked on, I sat watching the early morning sunlight dance over the waves. As they kept up their parade to my feet and back again, I suddenly was struck by the vastness and power of the ocean. It could not be controlled by man. It was so very constant. It was endless and had currents that could sweep me away. It was unchanging, and its force was immense. I could step into it deeper and deeper, as far as I would like to explore, yet it would allow me to float and rest on its waves when I became weary.

Here was an object lesson about God. I could go as deep as I wished in exploring the depths of his love, and when the currents of life or even his great power overwhelmed me, I could rest on his waves of mercy and grace. Just as Phillip Keller saw lessons about the Christian life in his sheepdog,[1] so was I seeing lessons in the steady roll of the ocean before me.

Fulfillment came as ocean before me.

It was so easy to see God in everything that surrounded us. It seemed that he had opened our eyes, and we could see teaching and applications even in the most unexpected places. We might be in the midst of a trip with our children to the Nauset Beach lighthouse, to watch the alternating red and white rotating beacon cast its gleam over the water, when there would be the sudden realization that this, too, was an object lesson. There were people far away in trouble and despair, needing to be saved, and it might be our light that would illumine their way.

Or we found him in the heavens. Jim had never seen a shooting star, so it was with anticipation that we sat on the deck one evening in August, watching the sky in hopes of seeing one. It was the time of year for star showers and, as there were no lights anywhere around and no clouds, the sky was as though someone had sprinkled diamond chips across it as far as the eye could see. Suddenly one shooting star after another streaked across the heavens, burning out as they did.

Perhaps this was a vivid illustration of what had happened to man when he was made in God's image and then, in his desire to shine on his own, had fallen and no longer showed forth God's light. It was a gentle reminder that we need to be watchful that we don't burn out, in our desire to shine on our own. We need to draw our light from God, who set all lights in their courses.

Once, when we were standing on a crest at the North Truro lighthouse, we noticed a group of people looking out to sea, exclaiming and pointing every few minutes. Whales were closer to shore than usual, and we were up high enough to see them. Soon there was a thin spout that rose into the air and then disappeared in the breeze. That was all we saw: a spout—and then nothing.

Again, it was God's gentle way of reminding us that we too might do something that will draw the exclamations of people, but like chaff—or in this case like the spout—it will quickly be blown away. Humility was the lesson of the day, the understanding that if anything lasts it will be because of God, not because we made it happen.

Vacations seemed to be when our Teacher had our full attention and when we were more focused on him, rather than on immediate work to be done. In fact, we could always count on something happening, just prior, that would ready us for our time away in the class of God's character and love.

Before he began seminary, Jim's company had told him that he could work two days a week during the school year and full-time during the summer. We had planned on Jim working until our trip to Cape Cod in late August. Those were *our* plans. God wanted to show us and many others else something different. The company needed to make layoffs just as the summer was beginning and Jim, being part-time, was in the first group to go.

The week before Jim was to finish work, I was just finishing up my school year. When I was in the school office, I was asked by several of the teachers what we would do for income. Considering that my pay, Jim's military veteran's benefit, and the allotment from the seminary would all cease for the summer, my reply was, "I have no idea. Do you?"

One teacher suggested that she ask her husband about employment in the engineering firm where he worked. He had told her that they needed someone for about three months, and they did not want to go to the expense of advertising a position of such short duration. I assured her that any help would be warmly received and then we parted, she with a mission and I with hope that it would be successful.

Tuesday was Jim's last day of work, and those there who knew our situation were concerned and asked what he planned to do. He had no plan and told them so, bravely adding, "The Lord has to provide something. He knows we have seven mouths to feed. He has never let us down and he's never too late."

At 4:30 p.m. (quitting time was 4:45 p.m.), the phone rang and Jim was asked to come in the next morning for an interview at the company where my colleague's husband worked! Not only had the Lord answered, but he had done it before Jim's fellow employees went home, so all would see that God is truly reliable and totally faithful. It was not just a matter of him meeting our need, but using our situation to show others his faithfulness.

This story could stop there and be sufficient for a few hallelujahs, but its epilogue is an especially happy one. When Jim picked up his final pay check, he was surprised to see that he had been overpaid. Jim quickly informed his boss of the mistake and waited while he went to straighten it out. Upon returning, he told

Jim that it was easier for them not to correct it—and to keep the overpayment!

Was it a coincidence that the extra money came when we needed it so badly? No; by then we knew there are no coincidences in God's kingdom, and we knew who was arranging everything.

So Jim began a new job for the summer. That company needed a draftsman for only those few months and, because he excelled at drawing, Jim was hired. However, it was only a few days until the company discovered that his skill as an engineer would be more valuable to them, and he began design work on the sewer, gas, water, and other utilities systems under the streets of Philadelphia's Market Street East Redevelopment project.

Another "non-coincidence" was that Jim had completed a required US Army Engineer course in public utilities several years prior, thinking he would never have use for that knowledge. No doubt Philadelphia is better off today because of Jim's work, and we were better off because of God's work!

On Cape Cod, seeing Jesus' presence everywhere and absorbing his teaching was pure joy. We could understand Peter, James, and John not wanting to go down off the Mount of Transfiguration. The words of the third stanza of "In the Garden" seemed so fitting:

> I'd stay in the garden with Him
> Though the night around me be falling,
> But he bids me go; through the voice of woe,
> His voice to me is calling.[2]
> —C. Austin Miles

Like them, we would rather have stayed but were called to go. So pack and travel home we did—but only after I prayed, as I was turning the key in the lock, that Jesus would see the desires of our hearts and bring us back again. And he did, for ten more years!

Each year, as we were planning our trip, it would become clear who was to come to Cape Cod with us for one of the two weeks we would be there. It is generally accepted that taking others on your vacation is a not good idea, for such an arrangement could interfere with your own relaxation and fun. However, there were accommodations for our family plus six others to sleep, so we would not be crowded. It seemed the most obvious thing to do, and we were very aware that this was a gift we should share.

It began simply enough. A teenage boy, whose parents had recently been divorced and who was staying with us, as well as and the teacher with whom we fellowshipped in Bible study, were invited to go with us the first year. In every year that followed, we asked the Lord to show us who needed a retreat as much as we did.

So began a parade of guests: the college young people from the church where Jim was the student assistant pastor, a young man who was experiencing difficulties at college and doubts about his salvation, missionaries who would not have had a vacation otherwise, and friends who just needed time in God's garden of love. There were even friends who felt comfortable enough to ask if they could bring another person along, like one who was going through an especially hard time of disappointment and trial in his own life.

The amazing thing about all of this was our children's reaction. Instead of looking at it as an imposition, they took an active interest in who would be the next people to fill the guest rooms. "Who's coming this year?" was the usual question and, if we didn't have a ready answer, they would suggest that we'd better get busy and find out whom the Lord had in mind.

As the years progressed and the house changed owners, God showed us, by faithfully bringing us back to that special place, that *he* had not changed. Only when it was sold a second time, to new owners who required the home year-round, did our annual sojourns there cease—just at the time our children were becoming teenagers and summer jobs and differing interests were emerging.

I am firmly convinced that our willingness to share our vacations had a direct bearing on God's graciousness in returning us there, year after year. It was, perhaps, the last great lesson from our time on the Cape. Thinking more of others than ourselves, and meeting their needs rather than grasping everything for ourselves, pleases the heart of God and results in blessings for our own hearts.

❧

Life in the Mixmaster continued for the remaining two years of seminary. School began again for all of us and, to add to the press of time, Jim now was student assistant pastor at Leverington Presbyterian Church. This is always great training for a future minister, but I often wondered why the rest of us needed more training in how to juggle an already overflowing schedule!

Jim's duties included leading the fifth- and sixth-graders as well as the college and career group, and that sometimes meant taking our children on Sunday morning and staying through the evening. They became experts in finding every nook and cranny in the church, as they were often on their own to explore while we were busy. This led to discovering the stash of cough drops in the choir loft, for the choir's use. It was a marvel how the five explorers never had a dry throat or cough!

Through decades of experience in church life, Jim and I have often wished that other congregations could be such shining examples of Christ's acceptance, love, and care. I have never decided who ministered more to whom there, we to them or they to us.

Right from the start, it was obvious that we had been led by God to a special green and wholesome pasture. When Jim had called and asked about doing his field education there, Pastor Jerry Ellison informed him that they did not have such an opening, but they would pray about taking him on. They did, and Jim was hired.

Rarely has a family been so welcomed and taken right into the hearts of a congregation. Jerry and Margretta, his wife, could not have been better examples of true servants and caring, loving people, and their congregation reflected it. Kathy was of the age to be confirmed, but distance and our schedule precluded her attending the midweek confirmation class. Somehow in his busy schedule, Jerry met every Sunday with Kathy alone, until she was prepared to stand and give her testimony as she professed her faith.

Kathy has since stood before that same congregation and shared her ministry as a missionary, supported by the very people who once heard a young girl say her life was completely the Lord's. One of the delights of the Christian's life is that God arranges events in such winsome ways.

It was not only Kathy who was so loved, but our other four children as well (even though Bill eradicated the Sunday school's entire candy supply by memorizing all forty-eight verses of Matthew 5, when his teacher promised a piece of candy for every verse that could be recited). There were always goodies at fellowship hour after church, and we never had to worry about tummies being empty at lunch time. Plates of food and cookies were often pressed into our hands.

At Christmas time, when I despaired that the family would ever see a Christmas cookie again, one of the women baked enough to feed an army, and we munched for weeks to come. That first Christmas at Leverington, the Callahans informed us that their house on Cape Cod was not available for the holidays, but they felt that the Lord had a wonderful gift in store for us at home.

Of course he did; one door is not shut without God opening another. The Sunday before Christmas, one handshake after another left checks in Jim's hand or someone would discreetly reach over and slip a check into his pocket. And to add the ribbon on it all, the company that had laid Jim off sent a $135 check for unused sick pay and a turkey for the coming holiday. Narberth Presbyterian sent a check for $270. Christmas could not have been merrier, and Dickens could not have portrayed it better!

Oh, we wrote thank-you notes, but the post office doesn't deliver to the One we knew was responsible for such goodness. It was truly a blessing to be in the keeping of such a wondrous Father, whose gifts and givers are of such wide variety and abundance.

There had been jobs provided, money to meet our particular needs, pleasure and beauty experienced and, best of all, his presence to be enjoyed. Could anyone ask for more?

> In the secret of His presence
> how my soul delights to hide!
> Oh, how precious are the lessons
> which I learn at Jesus' side! ...
> And whene'er you leave the silence
> of that happy meeting place,
> You must mind and bear the image
> of the Master in your face.
> —Ellen L. Goreh

Because we spent time with him in places like Cape Cod and Leverington Church, I trust that all seven of us bear more of the likeness of Jesus and have seen more deeply into God's heart.

CHAPTER 6

MUSIC IN OUR HEARTS

It is good to sing thy praises
    And to thank Thee, O Most High,
Showing forth thy loving kindness
    When the morning lights the sky.
It is good when night is falling
    Of Thy faithfulness to tell,
While with sweet, melodious praises
    Songs of adoration swell.
                    —from Psalm 92,
                        The Psalter, 1912

Shout with joy to God, all the earth!
    Sing the glory of his name;
        make his praise glorious!
Say to God, "How awesome are your deeds!"
                    —Psalm 66:1–3

GOD MUST LOVE music a great deal. Not only are the Scriptures full of references to his people shouting and singing his praises, or just singing for the pure joy of knowing him and his kindness to them, but the descriptions of heaven include a number of melodious events.

Later in our ministry, mission work also confirmed that God has given Christians a faith that expresses itself in joyous song and music. I have found no other religion where singing is a part of public worship—chanting maybe, but not the joy of hearts overflowing in song. As our journey progressed, so did our experiences of finding our Lord in the music of our lives.

When I sing, I often think of missionary Eric Liddell, who said that when he was running—head back, chin high, and wind in his face—he felt God's pleasure. I certainly could never say the same of running, but when I sing, it is much the same. There is a special closeness with God as I sing about him, and warmth fills my soul as I listen to music that seems fit for the halls of heaven. I want so much for people to know of him, what he does for his people, how much he loves—and somehow, I seem to express it best when I'm singing.

As far back as I can remember, God has blessed me with a soprano voice and a desire to sing. Choir had been a part of my life since I was eight years old. In college I not only sang in the glee club but, at the invitation of the music professor, I also sang in the large Methodist choir he conducted on Sunday mornings—and then on Sunday evenings in the choir at my own church.

But it was God who graciously arranged for singing lessons for a girl whose family's budget did not include expenditures of that kind. Oh, there were no formal lessons. He just arranged for me to be in the octet at the early Sunday worship service, where the other soprano was Anna Moffo, who was just beginning her operatic career. As if that were not enough, I was also seated next to her at choir practice. How could I *not* learn under *those* circumstances?

It was no surprise, therefore, that I was occasionally asked to sing at Leverington Church. Shortly before Christmas, I was approached by a woman in the congregation who had one of the sunniest dispositions I knew, though her eyesight was rapidly failing and she was almost legally blind. She explained that some women of the church had read portions of the Bible onto tape for her to use in devotions at home. She wondered if I could find time to record some songs for her as well.

Despite my busy schedule, how could I refuse such a request? But there were two problems: where would I record the songs, and who would accompany me?

When I went to school the following day, I mentioned my friend's request to the music teacher. His quick response to my dilemma was to suggest that, if I would travel to the Mennonite church where he was the organist, he would help me make the tape. On my first free Saturday, armed with a tape recorder and sheets of music, I appeared at the church, ready to sing a few songs. Both the organist and God had a whole lot more in mind!

The church was most unusual in its decor. One side of the sanctuary was clear glass, and the other had a stained-glass window of red and gold flames, depicting the fire of the Holy Spirit. In the center, a huge, rough wooden cross was suspended over the pews. As I entered, the swell of music coming from the tracker organ made my spine tingle. I slipped into a pew and listened to my friend practice. I could sense that this was not going to be just a recording session, but an experience with God himself.

We set about recording one song after another, and re-recording the ones that weren't good quality, until I thought my voice would give out. Just as I was ready to fold up shop, certain that I had infringed upon my friend's good will long enough, he suggested, "Why not give your friend a treat and record some Christmas carols for her? I'll play, and you can join in whenever you feel like it."

Two weeks prior, at a Christmas dinner at Leverington Church, we had closed the program with some congregational singing that included "O Holy Night." While I appreciated the joy and love with which they sang it, their rendition did injustice to what is best sung as a solo. Figuring we would soon be at a small church when Jim graduated, my heart longed to hear the strains of that particular carol filling a large sanctuary one more time. The days of large organs accompanying my solos would soon be over, but I had concluded that whatever God ordained was best and tried to put my longings behind me.

Now here I was, singing my heart out with a big organ without connecting my desire of that recent evening with what I was doing. At that instant, I heard the organ start to play "O Holy Night," and the organist nodded for me to join in. Just as I was starting to sing the chorus, it occurred to me that I was doing *exactly* what I had been longing for!

But something was missing, or so I thought. "Lord, there's no one here to hear it." At the moment I turned to let the music ring through the church, the setting sun shone through the clear west window and reflected off the red and gold glass in the opposite window. The effect was a stunning golden halo around the cross, awesome enough that there was a catch in my voice. It is recorded as a reminder forever, for in that wonderful moment came his whisper, "Sing it for *me*, alone."

Ah yes, God must enjoy music—almost as much as he delights in giving his children the desires of their hearts!

All future preachers need practice, especially one who was more accustomed to dealing with centrifuges and computer card equipment. Thus Jim was both delighted and a bit intimidated to be asked to preach at the Cedarville Presbyterian Church, in southern New Jersey, just before he began seminary. The whole family was to be involved: I was to teach a Sunday school class, the children would sing, and Jim would preach. We were a traveling three-ring circus!

The ride was a long one, with Jim rehearsing his sermon and the children practicing their song over and over again, in hopes of being real competition for the Trapp Family Singers. I couldn't help wondering how long it would be before their willingness to "make Dad look good" would wear thin. Much to my relief, we arrived before any insurrection erupted and were gratified to find that, while this was not exactly their idea of spending a fun-filled Sunday, their support and good humor were still intact.

As we made our way through Cedarville, we were reading all the church signs in hopes of landing at the right place. Suddenly a shout went up: "There it is! Look at the sign!" In bold letters, right under "Welcome Caldwells," were listed *all* our names as the visiting attraction. Jackets were straightened, dresses were smoothed, shoulders went back, and off they marched as if their careers were about to unfold.

Sing with gusto they did—and captured the hearts of the congregation! Somehow they had taken literally the words of their song, "Freely, freely you have received. / Freely, freely give."[1] It was obvious that they knew how much God had done and was doing for us all, for they sang enthusiastically, giving what they could in return.

On the drive home, they were recounting all that had transpired. Sue offered that the five of them had considerably swelled the size of the Sunday school, Bill and Dave commented that Dad's sermon illustration about a peanut butter sandwich was a little on the lame side and could use improving, and Nancy and Kathy wanted to know if they were always going to be included in the sermons. We listened to "Freely, Freely ..." being sung all the way home, with new and different variations being tested for their next engagement.

And a next engagement there was. We were invited back, and that time the invitation was extended to Jim "*if the children will sing*," a sure way for God to keep a future preacher's ego in check! After the service, all of them were interested in what was in the envelope that had their names on it. In the car, they opened it to find an honorarium for "Caldwell Singers," ensuring their future as the "best back-up" a preacher could ever have. It was fun seeing how God was keeping a family working together and showing our children that he was appreciative of both their efforts and the music they made.

❧

Just as heaven surely is filled with music, so was our home—though not with full choirs and perfect orchestrations, but with sounds from our piano. All our children took lessons, but any of them will tell you that no one held a candle to Nancy's musical ability. Even at two, she would dreamily conduct any music she heard, and, as the years progressed, it was apparent that God had gifted her. The others loved music but were happier listening to it than having to practice to obtain the desired effect. For Nancy, it was a love—and practicing, even though it was hard work, was not a chore.

Jim and I never could understand how she could coax the trills and runs from our modest spinet or memorize the many pages of music that were in her repertoire. This was especially amazing because Nancy had been born with the umbilical cord twice around her neck and was a frightening shade of gray when we first laid eyes upon her. It was a year before we relaxed and accepted that all was well with her reflexes and learning ability.

Then there had been the harrowing experience, when she was five years old, of her tripping on an escalator and her fingers starting to feed into the moving steps. Kathy, thinking Nancy was fooling around, gave her an impatient yank, which saved her fingers. A few stitches by a hand surgeon, who "just happened" to be in the emergency room, and her fingers were soon as nimble as ever. As we watched them fly over the keys, we never ceased to wonder at God's intervention.

Every one of Nancy's teachers eventually suggested that she needed to study with someone more qualified, until finally it was suggested that we seek the skills of Mrs. Gottlieb, formerly the head of the piano department at nearby West Chester University. I placed the phone call, never dreaming that we were jumping into a whole new world. Mrs. Gottlieb suggested that I bring Nancy for an audition. Audition? Caldwells didn't audition. We just took lessons!

Nevertheless, off we went. How else would we ever procure this lady's services? I sat and listened while Nancy played one piece after another on a grand piano, while Mrs. Gottlieb offered suggestions and corrections as she played another. After an hour, I stopped listening and started to do some mental calculations. We would be lucky to leave this one session without owing more than the national debt, let alone pay for lessons!

About then, Mrs. Gottlieb announced that she would indeed take Nancy as a pupil. Gingerly, I asked what we would be paying and how much this session had cost. Through my astonishment, it somehow registered that I was being told there would be no charge for the present time and we could pay whenever we could afford to. Amazingly, Mrs. Gottlieb was more interested in teaching a talented student than in money, and God was intent on finishing what he had begun when he gave musical ability to this child.

So began years of Nancy practicing, playing in competitions, and winning many of them—and hours of musical enjoyment for the whole family. Several years later, as Nancy was starting to think seriously about college, it was clear that God had other than musical plans for her. She was being called to be a teacher—not of music, but of history. It was hard for us to accept that the house would be quieter and, quite frankly, it was difficult to lay it all on the altar. What had been the purpose for all those years of lessons and practice?

Isn't it strange how we assume that excelling and success are so important to God? At that time, it didn't occur to me that maybe what he wanted most was for Nancy to enjoy her talent to the fullest. He might have been enjoying those hours of music as much as we were, even while he knew that she could best touch lives for him by doing something else for a career.

Today Nancy teaches history in a Christian school, where the lives of her students are affected by her example. Mother of three wonderful children, she makes fulfilling the purposes of God her priority, enjoys all things as they are given, and does not grasp fame or fortune for her own.

ॐ

God's timing is especially interesting when he somehow manages to match music and events. Try as we might, we could never manage to make it all come together as he does, in ways that show his glory and leave impressions that will forever be in our memories. The day before Jim's graduation from seminary was such an occasion.

We had come to the end of three years, worn out and panting as we crossed the finish line. It was the last week of school for me. End-of-school events and all the children's closing programs had been attended, my grades were due, there were Jim's baccalaureate service and Alumni Day concert to attend, graduation ceremonies and Jim's ordination service to celebrate, and we were to move to our new church the next week. Amid the packing boxes, Jim and I managed to find the proper attire for all of the events.

I really was quite astounded that Jim had enough adrenalin to drive yet another time to Princeton and stay awake through everything. I was too tired to focus, but I kept looking forward to the concert, where music would be a sweet escape for an hour. Joy Simpson, that year's artist-in-residence at the seminary, was to sing, so I knew there would be balm for my frazzled spirit.

Jim and I slid into a pew in Miller Chapel and let the sounds flow over us, but toward the end of the program I began reviewing all that had occurred and thinking about all of the people who had been a part of it all. Mom had gone to heaven several years before we had begun this amazing journey toward the ministry, and my mind drifted to thoughts of her. Oh, how proud of Jim she would have been! How pleased she would have been to see how her grandchildren had risen to all of the occasions that would have made most young people complain. How she would have rejoiced in watching how the Lord had met our every need. How very aware I was of the veil that separates us in death, for I wanted so badly to share it with her.

When overtired and somewhat sentimental, I suppose it is not unusual to want one's mother nearby. As my eyes filled with tears,

I ducked my head so those around me would not wonder at them spilling down my cheeks.

Just then I heard Joy Simpson announce her last piece, explaining, "This last song is not the kind of number to be sung at the end of a concert. I have sung before kings and queens and in many concert halls, and I have planned many programs. Normally I would leave you with a song that would be uplifting and joyous, but today I feel that the Lord would have me finish with a love song."

With that introduction, Joy began to sing "In the Garden," the song I had heard my mother sing every night in my childhood. As her last words softly filled the chapel, so did another voice speak softly to my heart, "Lois, your mother knows." There was One who cared about a frazzled, tired, sad wife and mother, One who could break the silence of separation and could lift a soul beyond all the pressures and send her out with a smile to replace her tears.

"To God be the glory, great things He hath done!"

Narberth Presbyterian Church was ringing with the music. The night of Jim's ordination had finally arrived. The children could hardly believe that three long years had passed, and they couldn't have been more proud as they filed into the front pew with us. Not only were they about to become PKs (pastor's kids) and their dad their pastor, but they well knew that they had been a major part of it all. The girls were in long dresses and wore corsages, pinned on by their dad. The boys wore coats and ties, and it would have been a challenge to find more proper gentlemen.

Jim and I vacillated between exhaustion, excitement, awe, and nervousness. The choir processed, all forty of them. Nothing had been left unturned. Our souls soared in praise! God had done it!

If I had my guesses confirmed, I would not be surprised that in all the music being sung were the voices of some angels, the ones God had sent to our aid so many times. Certainly the saints in heaven must have been singing along, for it hardly seemed that a congregation alone could produce the sound that filled that sanctuary. If ever the word "praise" needed a definition, it was found in every facet of that evening!

How grateful I was to be singing early in the service! I had to be nervous for only a little while before I could relax and soak in all that was transpiring. I was well aware that the words of my solo were right out of Scripture. They were God's words from Isaiah 52:7 (KJV), and I was his instrument to sing them for Jim. How fitting they were: "How beautiful upon the mountains are the feet of him that bringeth good tidings, that publisheth peace; that publisheth salvation; that saith unto Zion, Thy God reigneth!"

When a prayer finished, I took a deep breath and ascended the steps to the chancel. I turned around in preparation to sing, and in my astonishment nearly fell down the steps I had just walked up. The church was full from front to back, so was the balcony, and even the side overflow room had a healthy number of seats filled!

Where had all these people come from? I did a quick once-over and realized that there were missionary families from WEC, friends who had helped us over those three long years, almost the entire Narberth Church family, many from Leverington Church, family, members from the congregation that had called Jim to be their new pastor, and even Jim's co-workers from both his regular and summer jobs—including one Jewish friend, who knew no one else there but wanted to share in the glory of the moment with Jim. God had assembled the saints!

The organ began and joy filled my heart as I sang. At the words, "I will sing unto the Lord as long as I live," I determined to sing his praises for as long as he gives me breath, and I trust that my last song will be a song for him.

After the sermon, the charge was given, Jim was robed, and the last hymn, "Jesus! What a Friend for Sinners," began. What heavenly harmonies reverberated off those gothic stone walls as the chorus swelled, "Hallelujah! what a Savior!" I stood on tiptoe, the closer to be near him, and our hearts came near to bursting. And this was not the end, but only another beginning!

At the reception that followed, the children lined up with us to greet everyone. I treasure the picture of them, perfect stair steps in height, shaking hands as if they had been attending formal functions all of their lives. Only after two hours of greeting people and watching everyone else devour the refreshments, when some kind soul brought a plate of goodies for the children, did I hear Dave quietly comment, "Finally! I figured it'd all be gone before I was kissed to death!" Dave always did have a knack for stating the obvious and bringing us back to earth.

It was a night to be remembered by all of us, for in it we had experienced the glory of a Father who completes all things well, whom we could trust to see us into the future. No matter how long we travel this journey, it will be to the accompaniment of song and music in our hearts, and I suspect that many of our melodies will include the rich voice of Jesus, singing right along with us. Even when our voices become too weak to sing, he will hear and know the words we want to lift in praise.

> There's music in my soul today,
> A carol to my King.
> And Jesus, listening, can hear
> The songs I cannot sing.
> —Eliza E. Hewitt,
> "Sunshine in My Soul"

CHAPTER 7

AS THE STEEPLE TURNS

Be still, my soul: the Lord is on thy side;
   Bear patiently the cross of grief or pain;
Leave to thy God to order and provide;
   In every change He faithful will remain.
Be still, my soul: thy best, thy heavenly Friend
Through thorny ways leads to a joyful end.
      —Katharina von Schlegel,
        Trans. by Jane L. Borthwick

...now for a little while you may have had to suffer grief in all kinds of trials. These have come so that your faith—of greater worth than gold, which perishes even though refined by fire—may be proved genuine and may result in praise, glory and honor when Jesus Christ is revealed.
      —1 Peter 1:6–7

WITH A SENSE of high calling and clear direction from the Lord, we left for Jim to take his first call to a church. In fact, so clear was the call that we had delighted in sharing it with missionary friends. We had been a bit puzzled by their response, that a call so clear most likely meant that we were going to need to be very sure of it in the future. How naive we were, and how prophetic they had been.

Jim was installed as pastor on our second Sunday there and had his first meeting with the Session (the board of elders) the following evening. Not being acquainted with the usual length of Session meetings at that point, I was not too concerned until midnight approached and Jim still was not home.

When he walked in, he was sagging like a deflated balloon. Every seminarian is told that the first six months at a church will be a honeymoon between him and his new flock. But this honeymoon was over, not twenty-four hours after it began! In the absence of an installed pastor, a major issue had been tabled. Now, as soon as they had a pastor, it was brought up. Jim was caught in the crossfire.

Certainly things would get better.

It appeared so when, a few days later, we were invited to the home of the matriarch of the church for tea. How nice! We arrived full of hope and pleasantries and, in proper style, were served tea with little cakes. I never got past the first few sips of tea. Somewhere between the tea and the first bite of cake, I heard our hostess announce that *she* had been the Sunday School Superintendent for forty-three years, had been there a lot longer than any of the previous pastors and would be there long after we were gone, so it really didn't matter *what* Jim did in his ministry.

My choking fit that ensued was more a result of the words I had just heard than the tea scalding my throat. I silently gave thanks that Jim was the pastor, not me; my response would not have been nearly as studied or kind as his was. But little did we know how right that feisty lady was. It really didn't matter what Jim did. As Jim shook hands at the door every Sunday, she was standing opposite him as long as we were there, and even after we were gone, giving out candy.

Shortly thereafter, we were invited to a dinner at a Masonic lodge. Perhaps this was another chance to socialize and get to know people. As it turned out, all except five men in that church were Masons, and there were eight past grand masters and a present one in the congregation. Of course they assumed that Jim would want to join their ranks and ask entrance into the lodge. Jim kindly explained, to those who had invited us to the dinner, that this was not his intent. He already had taken the only vows he ever intended to take, those of his marriage and his ordination. He was committed to living a life openly before people and God and thus could not be part of a secret society.

That so many were Masons and at least one-third of the congregants were interrelated did not help the reception of Jim's decision. This boded no good for future relationships, but at the time we didn't realize the impact it would have.

Then there was the interesting meeting with the local police chief. The Sunday school building sat apart from the church and was rented for weekday use by a private school. The chief cordially invited Jim to lunch to get acquainted—and to tell him that the police had discovered that the school was for the children of members of a cult, which they were going expose. He felt it best to warn the church before the story hit the newspapers.

Thankful to be warned, Jim assumed that the matter was ended when Session terminated the rental agreement. Not so. There was more concern among the trustees over the revenue that was lost than for the integrity of the Lord's house. We began to wonder if we had heard God's call accurately.

Sometime in the midst of our confusion and bewilderment, Jim was visited by a parishioner who had a close, committed walk with the Lord. She had been reading that morning in Ezekiel, chapter two. She felt the particular passage carried no relevant message for her and had prayed about it, asking the Lord why it seemed so important and pressing. She told Jim that she felt the message was somehow meant for him. Deciding that two heads were better than one, he waited until lunchtime to read it.

That God was speaking so eloquently to our present situation, from words penned millennia ago, amazed us. They filled us with both apprehension for the future and a sense that God was aware of what we were encountering. He already had tested us in depending on him for our needs, but this was escalating to far beyond just financial needs.

What we read was immediately relevant, for it began, "Son of man, I am sending you to the Israelites, to a rebellious nation that has rebelled against me; they and their fathers" (Ezek. 2:3). The church bulletin cover proudly proclaimed, "Church of Our Fathers."

We read on. "The people to whom I am sending you are obstinate and stubborn. Say to them, 'This is what the Sovereign Lord says.' And whether they listen or fail to listen … they will know that a prophet has been among them. And you, son of man, do not be afraid of them or their words … You must speak my words to them, whether they listen or fail to listen … But you, son of man, listen to what I say to you. Do not rebel like that rebellious house; open your mouth and eat what I give you" (Ezek. 2:4–8).

Oh, it was abundantly clear. This was not going to be the wonderful experience we had envisioned. Whether or not they were rebellious, we certainly did not want to be, and that translated into Jim preaching the message of the gospel no matter what the reception was going to be. Being the proverbial optimist, I suggested that we read on into chapter three and see how this whole scenario was going to turn out.

Before and during Jim's time in seminary, we both had desired to serve as missionaries—and even had pursued it. Particularly, we had felt a burden for the people of Iran. The Lord had made it clear to Jim that he was to remain in the church, to show Christians who God really is and what he has for them. God knew the future, for we would have entered Iran just before the revolution resulted in almost all missionaries having to leave.

So now we were reading in chapter three of Ezekiel, "You are not being sent to a people of obscure speech and difficult language … whose words you cannot understand. Surely if I had sent you to them, they would have listened to you" (Ezek. 3:5–6).

We found no guarantees of future peace and happiness, only the acknowledgement that God knew what was happening and we were to be obedient. And so the passage concludes, "I sat among them for seven days—overwhelmed" (Ezek. 3:15). It was accurate, all right; we could not have been more overwhelmed!

Things didn't get any better. It wasn't long before Session voted to paint the inside of the church a soft Williamsburg blue and the trustees had it painted light green, as it always had been. Jim asked the presbytery how to handle the situation, only to be told that the trustees could not go against Session's authority, a regulation that Jim knew only too well. When he responded that it already had been done, the answer was another "They can't *do* that." By then, Jim was having trouble figuring out what part of "already has been done" was so hard to understand. To make matters worse, it was inferred that all of this was happening because of Jim's inexperience.

But certainly it was not his inexperience that caused the former pastor to return and visit eighty people in the congregation, providing them the guidance they sought to try to precipitate Jim's departure. Letters were written and passed out to all members after unpopular decisions by Session, and the gossip chain was so incredibly active that it was hard to believe that the walls were not listening and relating all of our conversations. If we sneezed in the morning, it was not surprising to be called by that afternoon and asked if we had a cold.

To make things more interesting, one woman called almost every time Jim left and asked me if I knew, *really* knew, where Jim was and what he was doing. In our better moments, when we could muster enough humor to laugh, we decided that we had landed in the middle of a soap opera and quipped that we could make a fortune writing episodes for a series titled "As the Steeple Turns."

Most of the time, however, we found no humor in the events which were swirling around us, and we tried just to endure each day with our faith and our family intact. Had we not had practice trusting God for our existence during those seminary years, I doubt we could have withstood the onslaught. We somehow still believed that God would rescue us, a hope that was getting harder to hold on to as the situation compounded.

∽

It had been only a few months and already Jim was entering into a state of clergy shell shock, and I was beginning to have chest pains. Being new to the area, we knew no doctors, so I let my fingers do the walking and found that God knew all about the Yellow Pages. He guided my fingers to one of the most knowledgeable and compassionate doctors I have ever met.

I was brought up short when, after he had examined me and pronounced that I most likely had an esophageal ulcer, he informed me that he was not surprised. He knew the reputation of our church, for he had treated a previous pastor! He also told me that I was depressed. Given that I was watching what was happening to Jim and the children, every diagnosis for stress, exhaustion, anger, and depression might well have applied.

While all five children were trying desperately to exemplify Christian behavior, they were utterly confused at how people could say they believed one thing and then act the opposite. After three years of seminary and years of support for their overloaded parents, they wanted to see us happy and at peace and having time again as a family. I was aware of their disappointment, but there was little we could do. I was aware, too, of the slurs they encountered at Sunday school and the names and nastiness they were enduring.

My only comfort was that they all attended Delaware County Christian School, where the love and godly atmosphere would make up for some of it. It was tempting to fold our tents and quit, but it was not that simple. There was the matter of obedience to a call of God no matter what the cost, and the cost was mounting to more hurtful and depressing proportions.

An anti-depressant was suggested by the doctor. My conviction was that I should be able to handle all of this with faith and more aplomb. I declined the anti-depressant with the excuse that Jesus had gone through a lot worse than we were facing, and he hadn't been in need of an "upper."

That excuse produced one of the shortest, most effective sermons I have ever received. Dr. Vossenberg slowly swiveled his office chair to face me. With compassion and a face that could not have been more serious, he responded, "Lois, *you* are not *Jesus*."

It's strange how truth so simply put can sink into the depths of one's soul. I got the prescription filled and began to see what, in later years, would help me counsel depressed clients who would come to me for help. The prescribed pills produced feelings of otherworldliness, which added to my unpleasant mix of emotions. (The more modern anti-depressants had not yet been introduced.)

Jim knew that the whole situation, which encompassed much more than I care to relate, was getting beyond him. The presbytery's Committee on Ministry soon realized that the congregation was not receptive to advice, so they called for an administrative commission to settle matters. This meant that the Session, Jim, or both could be removed. Of course, if Jim were to leave the church, our home, our livelihood, and much more would disappear, which did not fit the picture God had given us.

We were sure of God's call—or were we? By now, we weren't truly sure of anything except that God had kept us in the past and specialized in resurrections. There had to be *some* way he could breathe life back into us all.

The commission began by listening to everyone except us. Of course, the initial assessment was that Jim was at fault, being a novice pastor; never mind the history of unhappy pastors that was being ignored. It was another coal heaped upon our heads; although, in fairness, it would have been difficult for those not in the thick of it to ascertain the extent of the problems. It is always hard to believe that those who call themselves Christians can be so hurtful, couching their actions and talk in self-righteousness and innocence. It seemed as if no one heard, no one cared, and that God, if he had a plan, was indeed being slow about revealing it.

Even amid all that was swirling around us were signs that God was still leading. At Christmas, card after card contained this note: "We thought this verse from Jeremiah might encourage you—'For I know the plans I have for you,' declares the Lord, 'plans to prosper you and not to harm you, plans to give you hope and a future' (Jeremiah 29:11)."

A few kind and loving souls in the congregation, who were not involved in the furor, were the Lord's ministers to us. Lillian Hill mothered Jim with encouragement, proving that it is not blood that determines our relationship to one another but our relatedness to Jesus. And Jim needed mothering. He used to face Sunday's worship with a courage I have yet to uncover in others, but at home afterward, he drooped like a wet dishrag. Lillian was always there with some baked goods, a smile, and kind words.

There were others. Marion McCreary was truly the balm in Gilead. Being of practical nature, she would take the kids camping, take over when the burden was beyond me, and talk of spiritual things when the edges of my faith began to unravel.

We had promised our children that, when seminary was finished, we would take a trip to Disney World. We would make good on our promise, even if it took every last bit of our money and energy. The children were thrilled! They could leave the unhappiness at home and forget for a little while. Seeing their happiness revived us somewhat.

Our two-day visit to Disney World was the usual—spinning in teacups, being scared by pirates, oohing and aahing at Cinderella's dress, and screaming along with everyone else on the dips and turns of Space Mountain. We all were splashed at Sea World and counted the huge mating grasshoppers in the Everglades, swatting mosquitoes all the while.

George Callahan had been called to a church in Florida and, pastor to us that he was, had us come and spend the next week at his Pompano Beach home. And then it was time to return home, but not before George took us to the beach.

As the children were cavorting with Jim in the surf, George and I basked in the sun and talked about the situation we were going home to face. George commented that perhaps I should convince Jim to get out of this church and save him for the ministry. I'm sure my retort, "We can't just up and leave until God tells us to go," seemed a naive answer to his kindly concern.

Later, cleaned up and ready for our afternoon flight, George took us to lunch at the Lighthouse Point Yacht Club, a real treat and more opulence than the children had seen in years. Not one to be put off, George tried again, this time asking the children, "What do you think of what's happening to your father?" I could have told him not to bother; I knew the kids better than that. Ever loyal, they informed "Uncle George" that they were sure their dad would do whatever God wanted him to do.

Smiling to myself, I was silently blessing them for their love and trust in their dad when I suddenly "came to attention." A *bang!* on the table rattled the glasses and caused guests at nearby tables to stare. George exploded, *"Jim, you are either Jeremiah, Ezekiel, and Amos all rolled up in one, or you are the worst of fools!"* Jim and I had to admit that it did look that way, but the statement had God's voice in it, though George wasn't aware of it.

Back home, we were getting ready to go out for an evening, having told the children not to let anyone know where we were.

(Often there were phone calls, almost as soon as our car departed the driveway, asking the children what we were doing and where we had gone.) Shaking my head that I found myself giving such instructions, I teasingly called to Jim, "Hey Jeremiah, Ezekiel, and Amos. You'd better get a wiggle on, or we'll be late." No sooner were the words out of my mouth than I knew that God wanted us to look in the book of Amos.

We knew what God had said to us from the other two books, but what did he want us to know from Amos? Jim must have felt the same thing, for the next day he appeared at lunch with his Bible and announced that he wanted me to read a verse from Amos.

I was one step ahead of him, because that morning I had read that entire book, certain there was a relevant verse for us. We discovered that we both had come to the same verse: "Surely the Sovereign LORD does nothing without revealing his plan to his servants the prophets" (Amos 3:7).

This might have seemed a strange word indeed, were we not being blindsided by so many events that were happening. Suffice it to say that somehow, from then on, we always got wind of what would come next before it actually happened. Not that we could stop it or do anything about it, but we were never caught unaware. We could brace ourselves for what was to come and pray for wisdom in handling it.

God really hadn't forgotten us.

Our situation only seemed to be getting worse, and I was beside myself, holding onto the last knot in my rope. We needed help: someone to love us, believe in us, and minister to us. I would have turned up rocks to look for such people, but even rocks didn't seem to be there.

One Saturday night, while Jim was in his study at the church, struggling to put aside his own emotions so he could hear how God wanted him to preach the next morning, I literally fell to the floor and cried to the Lord, "We can't go on. No one knows what is really happening here: money getting put in funds so they can bemoan their financial 'deficit'; the hurts they inflict; the picture they are painting of an inexperienced pastor, wet behind the ears, when in truth Jim has had years in business and can see all too clearly what they are doing, and so can you. Please, please, send us someone, anyone, just someone who can hold our hands up like Joshua did for Moses. Please, Lord. We're trying to do what you want us to do, we're trying to stay, but we can't do it alone. Help us, please!"

Somehow I went to sleep, Jim finished his sermon, and the next morning dawned. Another usual day at church—*until*, as we were greeting people after the service, a new couple shook our hands and asked to talk with us. We met and shared, but we were careful not to talk about what was happening.

Three days later, Horace and Carol Lukens were back and asked what was going on, for they had been directed by the Lord to come to our assistance with prayer, encouragement, and care in any way we needed it. How does the Lord do those things? How had he answered so quickly? How had we ever thought he wouldn't supply our every need?

The bond that developed between us was something akin to a Jonathan-and-David relationship. Horace was a pastor's son and understood the workings of churches, and together they had experienced a very hurtful schism in their own past church life, so they understood all that we were going through. Every Sunday, they invited the seven of us to dinner. Our children could play tennis on their court and enjoy their two boys, while we could cry or relax and I sat in their big wing chair, hidden from the world.

Horace was a psychologist and knew when to cajole and when to bind up our wounds, and I never ceased to wonder at how closely Carol was tuned to my needs and the Lord's direction. I might be crying after the children left for school, when she would appear at the back door, knowing her presence was needed.

They attended meetings, praying in the background, but always there—where an apprehensive gaze from one of us was met with a smile, an affirming shake of the head, or an arm around a shoulder on the way home. And they stayed the course. Horace and Carol were there until God had truly granted us vindication and salvation from the situation and moved us to another place in his vineyard, one without bitter grapes. But that's getting ahead. The story goes on.

Following the Lord does not necessarily mean that all things will come up roses. Scars remain, even though the result is good. I suppose that is just one more reason why, when we meet Jesus, we'll be able to relate so well as his brother or sister. If we truly have followed him, we'll have scars, just as he does. But before scars can form, there are wounds—and the year ahead would bring more than we ever thought we could bear.

It was not a good year for any of us. Our two shining lights, Sue and Bill, would have their burning flames of faith severely tested. Sue was a straight "A" student, but her sixth grade experience was a disaster, because the teacher was emotionally abusive to the children.

Sue was mostly exempt, because she produced sterling grades, the only thing that seemed to please him. She was in a situation, though, where she could do nothing to help her classmates without inviting the same treatment for herself. In some ways the most sensitive of our children, Sue protected and nursed injured animals of any kind. Now she was being hurt more deeply than anyone that age should have to bear. It turned into a fierce determination to finish the year with a perfect record, so she could tell the man off.

My instinct was to storm the castle and bring heaping coals upon the head of one who would injure children so, but Sue begged me not to, because it would go hard for her. Much against my better judgment, I had to admit she was right, so I did nothing. The school administration could not yet see what was happening, and other parents were in the same dilemma I was. Who wanted to make things worse for their children?

Sue's grades would protect her for the few months until the close of school. Her goal of telling off the teacher was understandable, but I discouraged it as not being the most Christian response. She had worked too long and hard to have that perfect record taken from her. However, I could well understand Jesus calling the Pharisees whitewashed sepulchers and a generation of vipers.

The school eventually fired the teacher, but that experience was another of the hard hurts along our path. The effect on a charming, happy, sensitive child cut us deeply. Sue and I were both in the same straits—she by watching hurt inflicted by Christians at school, feeling so vulnerable and unprotected by those who should love her, and me by experiencing it both in the church and in the school situation. I can only surmise that Jesus saw it all and was weeping with us.

Bill had always been a fierce supporter of his dad, and watching what was happening was making him more cynical by the day. Both Sue and he had been confirmed while we were there, and they insisted on attending the annual congregational meeting. Relatives who were not even on the church roll were invited by some members to come and vote. The whole thing was such a debacle that when Bill arrived home, he slammed the door and announced, "If *that's* Christianity, who needs it?"

He was right. No one needed *that*; but *that* wasn't Christianity. What was needed was to see the life of Christ being lived out, and that was in short supply.

Could it get much worse? It would take a few more months before our Shepherd led us into safer territory.

The administrative commission called a joint meeting of Session, the Board of Trustees, and Jim, and the truth finally emerged. When asked what they didn't like about Jim, the answer was that they disliked his preaching. The examples they gave were two: they hadn't liked hearing about the blood of Jesus, which they found nauseating, and being led in silent confession before communion had made them feel guilty and ruined the whole experience for them.

Rev. John McCleary, who chaired the commission, walked home with Jim that evening after the meeting and said that he wanted to speak to our children. He assured them that this was not their dad's fault. He explained that the same thing had happened to Jesus, that sometimes when the gospel is clearly taught it is met with animosity. The children needed desperately to hear that, and I still remember the feeling of relief and gratefulness that swept over me.

A couple of weeks later, we were amazed when Reverend McCleary called to say, "Jim, I've been racking my brain for some way to get you out of there and save you for the ministry." True to his word, he masterminded arrangements for that church to pay Jim's salary and a housing allowance for a year after he would resign. This would meet our financial needs, so Jim could go back to Princeton Seminary to earn his ThM degree.

That year would allow Jim to seek another call and let God put him back together. However, we would have to move out of the manse, which meant finding short-term housing. Need I mention that finding a house big enough for seven, for only six months in case we should be called to another church, would be nigh on impossible?

Ahead was this new hurdle, yet another opportunity to trust God to get us over every obstacle. He did, which comes in the next chapter, but not before I was told by a woman in the congregation that she hated me. Alarmed that I had done anything so offensive as to produce such a blatantly hostile sentiment, I asked what I had done. The answer: "If you hadn't supported your husband, we would have had him knuckled under in three months." I was speechless.

I sorted out our belongings: things we would need for a change of seasons, clothes for each of the children to grow into, what we would need in the months to come and what we could do without. The piano was kept by our doctor and his wife, who occasionally took us out to dinner and helped in any way they could. Other things were kept by friends. The remainder had to be put into storage. We looked on as most of our things were crated and loaded on a flatbed truck. We wondered when we would ever see them again.

Jim really must have been feeling the uncertainty of it all. As we stood at the front door and watched the truck roll down the street, he put his arm around me and said with tears, "The day I married you, I promised to take care of you. Here we are, twenty-one years later, and you have nothing more than we did then, except you have five children to care for."

He was wrong. I had him. His arm was still where I loved to feel it most, around me. We had five wonderful children who loved us through thick and thin. Most importantly, we had the Lord—who was still in control and never stopped loving us, though it seemed that most others did.

Yes, we had experienced another truth about following Jesus: it can be costly. But one joyful footnote followed, twenty-two years later, when Jim called Reverend McCleary. "John, do you remember calling to tell me how you wanted to save me for the ministry? I want you to know that I'll be retiring this Sunday, after two long and fruitful pastorates. God really used what you did." There was rejoicing on both ends of the phone as John replied, "You've made my week!"

However, way back when we were leaving that church, feeling very much in shambles, I had no clue what God had accomplished by our being there. One thing I did know; I was adamant that I would leave the place better than when we had come and with some reminder of our presence.

Before we left, I planted red geraniums around the mailbox.

CHAPTER 8

IN THE DIAMOND MINE

When upon life's billows you are tempest-tossed,
When you are discouraged, thinking all is lost,
Count your many blessing – name them one by one,
And it will surprise you what the Lord has done.
— Johnson Oatman Jr.,
"Count Your Blessings"

I will go before you
and will level the mountains;
I will break down the gates of bronze
and cut through bars of iron.
I will give you the treasures of darkness,
riches stored in secret places,
so that you may know that I am the LORD,
the God of Israel, who summons you by name.
—Isaiah 45:2–3

IF ASKED TO describe our situation at that moment, we would have most likely described it as being in a dark pit. And if you are in a pit, the best thing is to dig, either to find your way out or for diamonds. The saying, "when life gives you lemons, make lemonade," seemed applicable. Scripture promises "the treasures of darkness, riches stored in secret places" (Isa. 45:3). So between crises, we started to think like the seven dwarfs.

As we began to dig through the mire and darkness, we were amazed at the gems we were unearthing. True, they were in their uncut form, but we could see God amassing treasure before our very eyes, at least when we put on the glasses of faith.

Later we realized that we had struck a vein of gold, for multiple situations unfolded that had to be either fiction or God-orchestrated events. As none of it was fiction, we could attribute them all to God and relish the times we felt rich in his love.

Most often we felt that love through others' warm actions, which came in extraordinary, sacrificial acts of provision, care, and hospitality. Such was the case with Marianna and Raleigh White. Marianna is one of the most giving people I know, and Raleigh is a dedicated, gifted plastic surgeon who sees far beyond the physical, to the deep needs of the soul. Both have a faith that sustains them so others can lean on them, and lean we did. We had known each other since Raleigh's days in residency and Jim's in seminary, so it was with great anticipation that we prepared to visit them in Texas.

The visit was a real respite for us because Marion, a teacher in our congregation and Mary Poppins in the flesh, was on vacation and had offered to care for the children.

We shared hours of good fellowship with the Whites and let them apply their own soothing brand of love. Here were people who could hear God speak and pass their encouragement and advice on to us, but more than that was to be received from their hands. Raleigh's practiced medical eye quickly saw that my pain was not only emotional, but also from the muscles in my back seizing up because of stress. I had valiantly tried to hide my discomfort, not wanting to dampen our happy visit, but squirming and shifting can escape a doctor's eye only so long. Though Jim had to return to Pennsylvania as scheduled, Raleigh successfully urged that I delay my return so he could arrange some physical therapy for me.

Reluctantly, Jim returned home alone, for school vacation was ending and Mary Poppins was about to depart on the shifting of the wind. I really needed the medical attention to my back—and a whole lot more, it turned out.

Raleigh made the necessary arrangements. Marianna lovingly drove me back and forth to the hospital every day, arranging her appointments, her housework, and picking up her children around my needs. I must not have been the easiest of house guests, because being waited on was a bit uncomfortable. I knew all about being more blessed to give than to receive, but I was having trouble *receiving* love in such portions, and our church situation had certainly not been conducive to learning that lesson!

Shortly into my visit with the Whites, we were all relaxing in the living room. I had kicked off my shoes and propped my feet up on the coffee table. My mother's "be a lady" came to mind. Had I heeded that reminder, my visit might not have turned out to be so lengthy, but then again, I might not be here to tell this story!

Sitting opposite me, Raleigh noticed the large brown birthmark on the sole of my left foot. I admitted that it had grown somewhat larger. After a close look, he insisted that he remove it, for the potential for it becoming cancerous was very real. I still ponder exactly how Raleigh "insisted." How does one insist in a gentle way and be forceful at the same time? (I'm still working on that one!)

We called home, Jim agreed that surgery would be wise, and Raleigh drove me to the hospital. Only a local anesthetic was involved, so in my naiveté I assumed I'd hop off the table and gingerly hobble around. I should have surmised what was coming when the nurse took me to the therapy room to learn how to use a pair of crutches! Raleigh had done a beautiful job of completing the surgery without a graft, having carefully pulled the skin together, but my foot would need gentle healing care and time. Home to the Whites' house I went.

If learning to be waited on was a new experience, having my wings clipped was much more so! I wanted to get this over with, to be healed yesterday and on my way back to Jim and the children.

But Raleigh and God were collaborating. Every time I asked Raleigh when I could venture home, he smiled and gave the same reply: "soon." Every time I asked God, his answer was "in my time." (I assume that he was smiling, too!) Either way, it was apparent that this was not going to be according to my schedule!

The whole experience was not without humor, however. Not being the most adept person on crutches (I never did like leaning on anyone or anything!), I periodically was responsible for adding gray to Raleigh's dark hair by falling or by tumbling down the stairs, threatening to undo all of his handiwork. Physical therapy still was required for my back, so Marianna now had the added job of getting me *and* the wheelchair into her car for our daily visit to the hospital.

One day, I hobbled into the wheelchair and waited to be taken down the long ramp into the building. Marianna turned to speak to one of her children, neither of us having remembered to lock the brake. She looked around just in time to see her friend disappear with accelerating speed. I was on a roller coaster ride down the ramp, hoping that someone would exit the sliding glass doors in time for me to go whizzing through!

Just a few feet in front of the doors I was about to shatter, a wheel caught in a crack and the chair veered into the bushes— upending me, the wheelchair, and my dignity in a heap. The resulting hilarity was the spoonful of sugar that helped the lessons of dependency and humility go down in such delightful (and comical) ways.

There were many talks with Raleigh over the few weeks that followed: talks about acceptance, perseverance, and reliance on God and not flirting with the idea of wanting to bail out. It all fit with the wisdom I was gleaning from reading the book of Job: to let God direct everything, even when the world seems to be falling apart.

When it was time to leave, as much healing had taken place in my heart as in my foot. With a copy of Kierkegaard's *Purity of Heart Is to Will One Thing* under my arm, I was finally returning home—with mounted longhorns for Bill's room and my faithful crutches.

As I boarded the plane, Raleigh took my crutches! He promised that I would be met at my destination with everything I would need. Suddenly I realized that all of my supports were gone! My friends would no longer be with me. Even my crutches, which I had despised at first and now saw as indispensable, had been taken away. There is a season for everything, and the new season demanded a purity of heart that willed only to continue following Jesus. The love of two precious friends had been the catalyst for my continuing on the path that would ultimately lead to God's heart.

It was Kathy's high school graduation, and then the autumn would bring with it enrollment in college and the beginning of thirteen years of college costs, sometimes with three or four children attending at once. Going through the seminary years had been just our kindergarten for learning to trust the Lord to provide! We were about to see what it was like to play in the majors!

Like every red-blooded American mother, I yearned to see my daughter properly fitted out for a good start. That would require a new bedspread, throw rugs, niceties to spruce up a dorm room, and some new clothes. Reluctantly those thoughts were pushed aside, and I hoped that the excitement of just going to college would be enough for Kathy.

My dreaming needed to stop. There was no money. It would be a miracle just to come up with the monthly tuition payments. As I let go of the dream of being the perfect mother, God stepped in and was the perfect Father, taking over in grander fashion than I could ever have conjured up.

The Whites called to ask for Kathy's initials. A few weeks later, a package of beautifully monogrammed towels arrived. Marianna had cleverly thought that a monogram on the towels would be a delightful way to distinguish Kathy's from others' in the school laundry.

A month before college was to begin, I received another phone call, from a couple who attended our church but were not members.

They were a childless couple of means, who had befriended us and been particularly kind to our children. They asked if they could give Kathy a graduation present, and would I be willing to accompany them and Kathy as they picked it out? Though I could not imagine why my presence was needed, I agreed to the offer.

Saturday saw Kathy and me seated in the back of their Cadillac, on our way to an extraordinary adventure. They gave Kathy the choice of three stores, two of which we did not frequent because they were beyond our pocketbook. The third was familiar only in that we usually visited the bargain basement there. It was a pleasure to hear Kathy choose the latter store, as I realized she had truly learned to be frugal and not grasping.

Arriving at the store, Kathy and I automatically headed toward the familiar bargain basement, only to be instructed that the specialty designer "shoppes" upstairs were our destination. This *was* going to be an adventure! We were directed to the coat department, where Kathy was asked to pick out her winter coat. She couldn't have been happier. Before that could fully register, she was asked to also choose a raincoat and an umbrella to complement it. Gulping, she did so, and we all proceeded to checkout.

Kathy could hardly believe what was happening when, instead of leaving the store, our friends went on to the next department. There she was told to choose a few skirts, one or two blouses, and a couple of sweaters. After that came a visit to the shoe department. We were both astonished. Our friends had been right to invite me along; this needed to be experienced to be believed! Kathy was just stunned. She had never bought that many clothes at one time in her entire life, let alone in the designer section!

An entire wardrobe was boxed and Kathy walked out of the store with both arms full of boxes, like some heiress from Rodeo Drive. It was Christmas in August and yes, she was an heiress: a daughter of the King, who had not forgotten her desires and exceeded in providing them through generous hearts.

A few weeks into the semester, Kathy called, laughing. It had struck her that she was attending college largely on grants and loans and probably was one of the neediest students there, yet she was wearing designer clothes and using monogrammed towels! What a sense of humor and love our Lord has! And what a valuable lesson for Kathy, whose future years in Christian-school teaching would require a tested confidence that the Lord would provide.

Later, when she and her husband entered the mission field, she could truly believe that their daily bread would be supplied by a loving Father. What a delightful way to begin her personal lessons of faith and supply. And what a wondrous way to remind a mother that, as much as we love our children and want to provide for them, they really are our Father's—and he will care for them better than for any bird of the air or lily of the field.

Our time at our first church was rapidly nearing its end. With trepidation, I scanned the rental ads for a home to which the seven of us might move. Week after week there was nothing that appeared workable. Despair was fast closing in when one lone ad caught my eye. One was all we needed.

It was a twin house with three bedrooms, fully furnished and available for five months. An immediate phone call disclosed that its owners were going to be away for that period, and it was immediately available for occupancy. I hurried to see it.

As I approached the house, I wondered whether it would hold our herd. Then, as I rang the doorbell, a great peace descended. By the time the owners opened the door, my skepticism had been replaced by absolute certainty that this was indeed where we would be spending the next few months. But how was I to convince *them*?

The Thompsons invited me in, and within a few seconds we were sharing our stories. The family was Roman Catholic, and Dr. Joseph Thompson taught political science at Villanova University. He would be taking a sabbatical to visit Northern Ireland and write a book about the conflict between Presbyterians and Catholics there. Great! Here was a Presbyterian pastor and his crew in need of this house, and that particular conflict was the subject! As I finished my story of why we needed to rent the house, our hosts simply agreed that the Lord would have us move there.

Expecting to sign a lease to make renting official, we asked for one. Again we were surprised when they declined by saying, "There will be no lease. We are your Christian brother and sister. Here are our bank deposit slips. Just deposit the rent each month." Northern Ireland needed this man!

While we were sitting in stunned gratefulness, they also offered to move some of their furniture to the attic to make space for a few pieces of ours, so our family would feel more at home. Joe offered to cart his books from his office in the basement over to the university, so Jim would have a quiet place to study and space for his own books while taking courses at Princeton Seminary. Suzanne volunteered to move her catering equipment to the attic, so there would be room for our boxes.

We prayed together before we left, and later we drove them to the airport and prayed again. They had understood our need, for their need was great as well. Later, when we were blessed with a monetary gift, we sent them a portion.

Again, we had to chuckle at how God does things. The Thompsons felt led to use the money we had sent toward a memorial window in their family's Catholic church in Ireland. I'm sure the whole affair was an object lesson in Christian brotherhood, and in Ireland there probably are still people pondering how a Catholic could trust that his home would not be blown to bits by a Protestant. And somewhere, in a small village, is a Catholic church with a memorial window partly provided by Presbyterians!

The house had bunk beds in the girls' room, the boys' bedroom barely had space to turn around, and Kathy slept on the sofa bed in the living room when she visited from college. Yet God knew precisely what we needed. Only the dining room was big enough for us all to congregate, so we spent time there every evening—catching up on each other's events, reading books together, sharing, and laughing.

It was that closeness which was needed to knit us back tightly as a family and start the healing process. No one even seemed to mind the long freight trains that rumbled by and nearly jolted us out of bed, and the girls still talk about the new spreads that made their beds special and inviting.

Even Christmas was special there. When I had been picking and choosing what to bring and what to leave behind, I realized that we would be there over that holiday and had randomly picked one box of Christmas decorations to bring with us. Upon opening it, "what to our wondering eyes should appear?" a red Christmas tablecloth and just the right decorations for the mantel, enough to make the place warm and cheerful and add just the right flavor for the season!

I often wonder what angel directed the choosing of that box!

New Year's Day was approaching, so our time in the Thompsons' home was fast coming to an end. Dilworthtown Presbyterian Church was considering calling Jim to serve as their pastor, but the pulpit committee had not yet decided, and we needed to vacate the Thompsons' house by January 3rd. Our entire family had prayed and felt the Lord calling us to Dilworthtown, but the committee had not yet heard the message clearly. What to do? Find another place to live.

Again I began searching the rental ads, an activity that was by now too familiar and distasteful. Again, one ad appeared, this time for a ranch house with four bedrooms. Jim wanted to wait until Dilworthtown let us know definitely, but all I could visualize was our family pitching a tent in the middle of winter. The departure deadline was getting too close for comfort.

One evening, so the children would not see our concern, we took a short drive to talk things over. Jim was certain that we were to be at Dilworthtown. I asked where we would live if the church never heard from the Lord that we were supposed to be there. His answer was simple: "Honey, if they don't call us, I have a bigger problem than where we're going to live. I *know* we're supposed to be there; so if they don't call us, that means I can't hear the Lord, and that means I have nothing to preach."

Well! How's that for a show-stopper? I had to agree that he was right, and he had to agree that we needed a place to live. That meant signing the lease for the house we had found.

As we bent over the six-month lease with pen in hand, Jim commented that he didn't feel right about doing this. I agreed with him, but what were we to do when our back was to the wall? We signed. In the days that followed, we painted rooms, cleaned the place within an inch of its life, cleaned the recreation room again after the oil burner spewed soot all over, and arranged to have all our things delivered on January 2nd. It was settled; we would not be needing tents after all.

On New Year's Eve after supper, the phone rang. The pulpit committee of Dilworthtown Church was calling to tell us they had met that evening (what church has meetings on New Year's Eve?) and had voted unanimously for us to come. Of course we accepted! We had felt the Lord's confirmation long before, when we had prayed as a family. It just had taken awhile for the committee to get the message. We went into warp speed, canceling the moving truck early January 2nd, undoing the order for turning on the electricity, and canceling the oil delivery.

It was reasonable to ask for the lease to be cancelled, considering that we had never lived in the house, had painted and cleaned it, and had managed to deal with the oil burner. The answer was "No"; they were going to hold us responsible for the full six months. This really distressed us, especially because these were Presbyterians and obviously at least *some* grace could have been extended. Oh, for our gracious Catholic brother and sister!

Thankfully, Dilworthtown Church paid the lease and we were free of that burden, but what a lesson in ecumenism and Christian witness. I heard Jesus asking, "Which of these … was a neighbor?" (Luke 10:36). The other lesson, which rang loud and clear, was to wait for the Lord. No matter how long he takes, his provision is never too late!

❧

Dilworthtown Church would need six weeks to spruce up the manse. But where would we live for those six weeks until the manse was ready?

Back to the ads I went, though by now we knew there would be nothing to rent for six weeks, and a motel was out of the question. Then I remembered seeing, in the Delaware County Christian School newsletter, that a couple had offered to share their big home. Their large family was all grown, and they were alone in a huge Dutch-colonial house. I called and received a warm invitation to come and see whether their accommodations would be satisfactory. At that point, a hen house would have looked inviting!

Betty Evans welcomed me warmly. The house was so large that each of the children could have a private bedroom, although they elected to share. It could not have been a more inviting home, with its game room and ping-pong table and plenty of space to spread our wings. I accepted on the spot and went back to gather our things and the family.

The Evans were some of the most gracious people ever to take in strangers, and a family of seven at that! It was arranged that I should do the cooking for us all, and we would all do our share of keeping the place clean and neat. Betty was a ham-radio operator and was learning Morse code, which fascinated the children, as did the player piano in the game room.

It was a good time and a warm friendship developed, which has lasted for years. It also was not far from Dilworthtown, which meant we could watch and delight in the changes that were being made to the manse. How happily things had turned out!

Progress had been made: we had learned not to ask "why?" but rather "how?" It didn't matter why; God had his reasons. Our part was simply to watch how God would deliver and then follow closely.

God included unexpected twists in the ways he wished us to follow. When we arrived at the Evans' home, we must have looked like a small circus: two cars, six people, a dog, and a moving truck.

I gingerly approached the house, realizing that we were enough to scare the bravest. At least I had met Betty, and she knew the number in our parade, so perhaps she would not be so overwhelmed. I rang the bell. It wasn't Betty who answered but Don, her husband whom I had never met!

Taking a deep breath, I said in my most charming voice, "Hello! We're the Caldwells. Uh—where would you like us to put our things?" Oh my, this had to be a scene out of a comedy production! I think I closed my eyes and prayed hard as Don's eyes went past me to the entourage in his driveway. I needn't have worried, for God had prepared the way. I was immediately wrapped in Don's welcoming arms.

We had made it! We had been digging in the pit, but oh, the gems we had unearthed! God had given us treasures in the darkness and riches he had stored for us in secret places: love, care, generosity, sacrifice, trust, unity, and hospitality. Could we have been richer? Perhaps similar experiences were what Dr. Raymond Edman had in mind when he titled his book about the Christian walk, *Not Somehow ... But Triumphantly!*[1] We hadn't just muddled through. We would arrive at Dilworthtown *triumphantly*!

CHAPTER 9

GREEN PASTURES

Oh, the unsearchable riches of Christ,
    Freely, how freely they flow.
Making the souls of the faithful and true
    Happy, wherever they go.
          —Fanny J. Crosby

Do not call to mind the former things,
Or ponder things of the past.
Behold, I will do something new,
Now it will spring forth;
Will you not be aware of it?
I will even make a roadway in the wilderness,
Rivers in the desert.
          —Isaiah 43:18–19, NASB

OUR SHEPHERD WAS taking us to new pastures, which we hoped would be greener, although by this time we wondered whether any church experience would be a place of peace. The "new" part we could understand, for we watched the manse being redone with thoroughness and love that was being extended from the whole church community. Even so, it would be awhile before we felt safe.

The manse was a historic house almost a hundred years old, situated on the site where the Revolutionary War's Battle of the Brandywine had ended. We already had our fill of living in a battle-field, so we concentrated on marveling at the changes underway to make this house a pleasant home and a place of healing. The congregation resembled a swarm of worker bees: some scraping years of paint from baseboards, others framing closets to take the place of the peg hooks where capes and gowns once hung.

What kind of kitchen did I want? Actually, any kind would do just fine if I would be the sole chef and could turn around without tripping over children. I wondered what they had in mind for choices and went to scout the existing kitchen before giving my answer.

Walking in the back door, I proceeded through the enclosed, heated porch and into—oblivion! There was not one thing in what should have been a kitchen. The stove, sink, refrigerator, and all the cabinets had been taken out and carted away.

Ron Barkman, the overseer of the project, stood there smiling and asked, "So what do you want us to put in here?" I didn't know him well enough at that point to hug him, but with wonder and overflowing gratefulness went with him to choose the furnishings for my new grazing grounds. This *was* going to be a new pasture!

In the ten years that followed, there wasn't one day that I didn't look up to admire the cabinets, appreciate the dishwasher, enjoy the new stove, or delight in the warm atmosphere that only the scents of dinners and baking cookies could improve. Evidently others thought so, too, because many chats were held with parishioners as they sat on the kitchen stool while I cooked.

Those kitchen walls listened to the tears of a father whose wife left him and two young children, concerns that work would be available after being "downsized," parental concerns over teenage children, joys over the great ways God was moving in lives, many missionaries' tales of their work overseas, and the beginning calls of some to follow in their steps.

❧

Jim was busy, but this time it was a good busy. The church services were exceptional. There were several well-established house churches, where weeknight meetings offered opportunity to share and encourage each other in faith. People became more and more intent on serving, some taking in those who needed homes and others carrying their faith more openly into the workplace.

Oh, surely there was still work to be done. As Jim was driving to a meeting with one of the elders, he was asked why we had not just up and left our previous church. Jim shared that had he done so, it would have meant leaving our livelihood, our health care, our home, our church, and our call from God. The elder whistled and replied, "Wow! I'm glad I'm not in your position, where all you have to fall back on is the Lord!"

Those words have been speaking to Jim ever since. That was the work to be done: convincing people that the Lord was really to be trusted in all things, was true to his word, faithful in every way, and was powerful and compassionate beyond our wildest imaginings. The challenge was *how* to help the Lord's children to test his faithfulness and thereby develop deep trust in him, when most of them *did* have so much else to fall back on. Years later, at our next church, Jim would seize upon mission trips as a means for believers to experience "all you have to fall back on is the Lord" and to find him fully able and totally faithful. They would—many for the first time.

❧

Praise, teaching, and prayer were the center of the house church meetings. One night there was a new face in one of the groups, a man who sat and listened intently. After the meeting, he asked if someone could take him to a job interview, because he had no car. Jim offered.

The next day, on the way to the interview, I said something about Jim being the pastor. Evidently no one had referred to Jim as such during the previous evening's meeting, so our guest looked aghast, mumbling something about being amazed that we wanted to be seen with the likes of him. As the conversation continued, we pieced together that he had recently been released from prison and had no job and very little money. He successfully landed the job, and we invited him home to celebrate.

By this time, our children were fairly well accustomed to sharing their dinners with a variety of people, but that night they were truly rendered speechless as they heard our new friend's tale about his time in jail. He had been caught in an armed bank robbery. Being an obstreperous sort, he had caused enough conflict in prison to be put in solitary confinement. One of the children regained enough composure to ask, "What did you *do* for all those months in solitary?"

He explained that he had read the Bible for lack of something better to do, but he had many questions about it that had not been answered. As dinner was nearly finished, and a more subdued gathering of children around our table I had not seen, I suggested that our friend first have a talk with Jim and then come to church and find the answers he had been seeking. Jim and he shared, and we wondered if we would ever see him again.

Like most churchgoers, Presbyterians have habitual pew space, and mine had come to be in the second row. As I was settling in, one of our children did a little rubbernecking to see if our dinner guest would appear. Then came a whisper that he was indeed there, two rows behind us. The service progressed with a whole pew full of prayers going heavenward that he would be comfortable among us and God would answer his remaining questions.

Prayer rails are not often found in Presbyterian churches, but every Sunday in ours, as a hymn was sung, people would come to kneel and make their petitions to God, trusting that Jesus would hear and answer. It was a double-sided prayer rail, so an elder could kneel to hear each one's concern and then pray, giving assurance that God would answer.

Just as we began the third stanza of Charles Wesley's hymn, "And Can It Be That I Should Gain," I noticed our friend departing his pew and thought the church experience had been too much for him. We were singing,

> Long my imprisoned spirit lay
> Fast bound in sin and nature's night;
> Thine eye diffused a quick'ning ray,
> I woke, the dungeon flamed with light;

His departure was not from the church, but rather from a life left behind in exchange for the Lord's goodness. He knelt at the prayer rail to ask for a new beginning and to commit his life to the Lord, just as we finished with these words:

> My chains fell off, my heart was free;
> I rose, went forth, and followed Thee.

Our hearts soared! The words of the refrain were so true: "Amazing love! How can it be …?" Could God have such green pastures? He had led us carefully to where we were a part of his great plan for redeeming people, and we were getting closer and closer to his great heart.

Even in green pastures, less enjoyable ways of getting closer to God's heart and understanding him are also encountered, for wolves enter there, too. At this point we were firm in our belief that our Shepherd was strong enough to fend off any foe. What we were about to experience, however, would lead to deeper understanding of both his power and the fellowship of his sufferings (Phil. 3:10, NASB)—an unpleasant learning time, but one of great depth and growth.

It was at that same prayer rail that Jim noticed a woman of our congregation coming forward for prayer on many Sundays. Her husband never attended, but she and her two children were there faithfully. We wondered what could be so critical, but she never offered to share details until one night, when she appeared at our back door with her children, seeking shelter and medical help. Her ear was bleeding where her earring had been pulled out, and she obviously was frightened.

We settled her and her children into beds. As I stopped to pray with her, she told me that she had run from her abusive husband, who was involved in illegal dealings. It had been a life of turmoil, and she had decided to seek a divorce from him, so she and her children could have a peaceful life.

Over the next few weeks, as the situation evolved and seemed to get murkier by the day, she asked if we could be present at court to support her young daughter, who was going to have to testify. That was out of our usual ballpark, but we consented.

As we sat with her daughter in the corridor outside one of the county courtrooms, we were aware of a whole contingent of people who were unknown to us but kept milling around, one repeatedly walking within inches of our toes. It was disconcerting, but we busied ourselves playing games and chatting with the daughter until she was called into the courtroom to testify.

Time passed, and finally the doors opened and she emerged, crying. As I raced to take her in my arms, I was intercepted by a man advancing at me on a direct collision course. Having just had breast surgery, my arms reflexively went up to protect myself. I was dumbstruck by the man falling down backward and yelling at the top of his lungs, "She hit me! She hit me!" With that, all the unknown people came to life, shouting that I had struck the man. I was baffled, speechless, and overwhelmed. I hadn't laid a hand on the man, and here he was putting on an act that would have done Broadway credit!

The courtroom erupted with tipstaffs, lawyers, and everyone else who could squeeze through the door to where we were. I looked around and the man had disappeared. Things settled down, and I decided that courtrooms were not to my liking.

Had it ended there, it would have been confusing, to say the least, but there was nothing confusing about the summons I received the next day, to present myself at court. I had been charged with harassment! To add spice to the whole affair, I had to post bail! As we had no extra money lying around, one of our elders graciously did the honor, if that's what one can call it.

Now began the challenge of finding a lawyer to represent me, having no money and no witnesses. I called my brother, Bob, who always seemed to be there when I needed him, and asked if one of the attorneys he retained for his firm might help me. After only a few hours, he called back to say that, from the information I had passed on to him about the man in question, his lawyers advised me to plead guilty!

My accuser, the man who had shouted, "She hit me!" in the courthouse corridor, was the father of the husband about whom we had been to court. The lawyers' thinking was based on the husband being well-known for his questionable connections, a person not worth fighting to keep from paying a fine. Could this be real?

It was not the fine I was upset about. I simply would not say I was guilty when, in fact, I was completely innocent. God had to be bigger than an easy escape with my pocketbook mostly intact and my honesty in shambles. He just had to be!

When the case was explained to a local lawyer, he agreed to represent me pro bono, which must have been arranged by the One in the place of highest authority. It finally was scheduled to come to trial months later, after enduring the harassment of having our phone tapped and people appearing at our door at night, wanting to "discuss" our parishioner's case. For once I was glad that our dog was antagonistic toward strangers and his threatening antics could well put off an army of men.

Not wanting to be tripped up in questioning after so many months of waiting, I returned to the courtroom. With sinking heart, I realized that I had no witnesses and still a confused recollection of the whole fracas.

As I was trying to recall the details of all that had transpired, I noticed one of the tipstaffs and asked if she by any chance recalled the incident. Much to my surprise, she did—and agreed to testify in my behalf, labeling it "the biggest setup" she had ever seen.

When it became known that I had a witness, a very credible witness, the case was dropped. My accuser's goal obviously was to intimidate me and make the cost high enough that we would stop supporting our parishioner. That hadn't happened, but my blood pressure must have suffered an altitude change and I seemed to have aged a few years, even though some very valuable insights were gained.

This all culminated the week before Easter, so I appreciated a little more of what Jesus had endured. I could better understand what it is to face the world of "law," where there is no forgiveness or grace. I now knew what it was like to stand innocent and be charged with sins not committed. I knew the sting of trying to convince people of that innocence when there was no tangible proof; standing silent in the face of accusers is sometimes the only thing left to do. Trusted friends had suddenly been "busy" or otherwise occupied, so now I could understand Jesus' hurt when none stayed with him and Peter denied him.

Easter was more precious after fellowship with Jesus on a Calvary path. I loved him even more and felt an even closer bond, not just because he had rescued me once again, but because we had walked heart-to-heart, sharing some of the same things that life had dished out.

The area was farmland when we first arrived at Dilworthtown. We had made our acquaintance with the cows that occasionally wandered across the road, and we delighted in the quiet setting. Down the road from the church was a small lane, which came in handy when a full house and the hustle of activity precluded private talks between Jim and me. The memory of one such talk still produces smiles.

Jim and I had bundled up and driven to that lane, to have a discussion where there would be no phone interruptions or need to respond to homework questions. We were far enough away for some privacy and still close enough to keep an eye on the house. Deep in conversation, we were startled by a knock on the car window and a flashlight beam in our eyes. Jim rolled down the car window, to be asked by one of the local police officers what we were doing.

We felt like two teenagers as Jim explained, "Sir, do you see that house next to the church down the road? Well, I'm the pastor of that church and there are five children in that house. We have escaped out here to have a quiet talk." The answer was quick and to the point: "Sorry, sir, I didn't recognize you, and I understand. I'll be leaving you alone now to enjoy the quiet. Have a nice night." As he drove off, Jim and I exploded in laughter. It made us feel young and whole again and put smiles back on our faces.

Life was full. In addition to all the church activities, family life was in full swing. I had major surgery and, for the first time during a convalescence, experienced care from a congregation that brought food, planted my flower garden, and otherwise showered me with love.

Graduations of every description occurred during those years: junior high, high school, and college. One year, three of us (including me, who had gone back for my graduate degree) wondered if the schedule would allow us all to attend each other's graduations!

There were Sue's art shows and Nancy's piano competitions and some of Bill's soccer events. And there would have been Dave's tennis matches to attend, except that he asked us not to come because it would put pressure on him. There were college interviews and moving into dorms, all of which had to be carefully scheduled so as not to overlap each other or move the right student into the wrong college.

All this, with either three or four children in college at once, amounted to long nights of filling out financial aid forms and searching the budget, again and again, for needed funds. By now, we did so with a lot more assurance that God knew every detail and would be answering our requests for help. It was a matter of sitting tight and watching the creative way he provided for us each time.

For Sue's coming wedding, we also had parts to play. Sue applied her artistic ability to put together a beautiful Victorian wedding, insisted on only family at the reception, and arranged for a friend to do the photography. I pitched in and made the bridesmaids' velvet skirts, and Jim presided over the wedding service, all of which added up to a delightful and elegant day. We hadn't needed bride magazines or wedding planners; we had a more heavenly pattern to follow.

∽

Kathy was also cared for in Jesus' special way. As she was approaching graduation from college, we were eleven hundred dollars short for her final tuition bill. There was just no way we were going to conjure up that kind of money.

Looking around for what we could sell, I realized that the only things to possibly bring in a few dollars were some Hummel figurines. We had given them to Jim's mother when we had been stationed in Germany and, after she died, Jim's dad had returned them to us. They were the only ones that hadn't suffered breakage from hymnbooks falling and balls being thrown.

I gathered them up and visited a gift shop owned by one of our parishioners, hoping that Betty would take them on consignment. She agreed to, though she warned me not to be too optimistic, as we were in a recession and she had not sold a Hummel for months. Not very hopeful, I drove home and opened the back door to hear the phone ringing. I was surprised to hear Betty's voice.

She informed me that a man had driven into the parking lot *as* I was pulling out. He had asked whether she happened to have one of the original plates that had been made by Hummel, in 1970. *Bingo!* There among the Hummels I had brought her, nestled at the bottom of the box, was that very plate! We had originally bought it in 1970 for twenty-five dollars, and I figured a hundred would be more than I could expect. How did *seven hundred and fifty dollars* sound to me?

Oh my! We were suddenly much closer to having what would be needed to spring Kathy from college. It never entered my mind that God would let her get this far and not finish the job, but we had three hundred fifty dollars more to go, and colleges have a way of not graduating those who don't ante up.

Three days later, Kathy phoned in the middle of the day—despite the strict rule in our family that all long distance calls were to be made after eleven at night, when rates were lowest. I waded right in, reminding her of the rule and asking why she would be calling on prime time when we didn't even have enough to pay her tuition.

When I came up for air, Kathy informed me that she had gone to her mailbox that morning and had found a cashier's check for four hundred dollars, with an anonymous note that the sender had been praying and felt the Lord directing her to send this gift to Kathy. The person mentioned that I had helped her sometime in the past, and this was just a little "thank you."

Here it was again: bread which had been cast upon the waters was coming back with jelly on it! We now had the eleven hundred dollars for the tuition, but why fifty to spare? It was only a few more days until Kathy was informed that the diploma cost twenty-five dollars and the cap and gown another twenty-five! God really does arithmetic precisely! As we sat at Kathy's graduation, we shared our pride with the unseen guest who had arranged every detail.

With five teenagers driving and many events to be attended, it was good that the manse was next door to the church and Jim could walk to his office. When a car broke down, though, it was a happening of major proportion. That happened frequently, as the cars we owned were not only pre-owned, but well-used. Jim's "second job" was staring at the underside of cars and thanking God that his engineering experience enabled him to keep our wheels turning.

But all good things do have endings. One of the cars died. There were tuition payments due and no possible way to buy a car—or even a used pair of skis or a sled or two. We were dead in the driveway!

After our "memorial service" for our departed car, Jim secluded himself in the study to ponder what solution he might turn up. I sat at the dining room table, watching the snow fall as quickly as my spirits, uttering the one prayer that seemed most used in these situations: "Lord, help!"

A knock at the back door roused me from my dejection, and I wondered who could possibly be coming to our door on such a snowy night. There, shivering in the cold after walking a half mile from her home, stood one of our parishioners. I hurried her in and asked what the matter was. "Oh, nothing. I just need to ask you something. My brother recently died and left us his car. We don't need it, and I wondered if *you* could possibly use it."

There are few times when I am rendered speechless, but once in a while God's amazing ways of doing things had just that effect! When I regained my senses, I informed her that we most certainly did have a need and inquired how much she wished us to pay for it. "Oh, I thought we'd make it a gift, or you could pay us a dollar." Even in my flummoxed state, I knew we could afford *a dollar*. Jim appeared, informing me he had not come up with any solution, just in time to hear that God had.

"Big Red," as we named the huge, bright red 1972 Mercury Marquis, had a few things to be fixed, but it was the perfect car for teenagers to be driving. We never had to worry about a small car in an accident; only a tank could have given more protection.

Considering all that had been showered upon us and all the times and ways by which God had delivered us, we thought he had done far more than enough. However, his goodness is truly never-ending, and once again he was arranging things before we knew we needed them.

At a doctor's appointment shortly before Christmas, Dr. Frank Vossenberg inquired about the children. He asked about Bill's interests, and when I told him that Bill yearned to ski and commented on the unlikelihood of him ever doing so, Frank further inquired what size shoe Bill wore.

A week later, after finishing his rounds at the hospital on Christmas Eve, Frank appeared with skis, boots, and poles, for which his son had no further use. Bill's delight knew no bounds! On went the skis and, much to our consternation and amusement, he proceeded to try them out by walking around the house with those six foot boards on his feet!

It had been an extra forty-five miles for Frank, after a day in the office and hospital rounds, and he had taken his Christmas Eve to make a teenage boy happy. It was not Santa who had appeared, but rather Christ in a good doctor's heart.

Small things also happened that made our children feel special. They often felt that we were lagging behind the times, because we couldn't afford the new things that graced many of the homes they visited. Mind you, there was no complaint, but when our covenant group gave us a microwave oven, our children exulted that we *finally* had entered the twentieth century world of technology. Amid the hoopla and scrambling to push the buttons, every conceivable thing was cooked or thawed in our new contraption!

What was happening on the home front was only surpassed by what was going on in the church.

Jesus had a reason for sending his followers out two by two (Mark 6:7), because they would need the support and fellowship of each other. Hence we gathered a covenant group, six couples including us, who committed to encourage each other to follow the Lord faithfully—wherever he would lead and whatever he would ask of them. Vocations would change and paths, of which only Jesus knew the destination, would be walked.

David and Lee Hall had come to Dilworthtown Church seeking a serious walk with the Lord, and he met their desire. They were the first to commit to mission service, which meant selling their house and moving to Columbia International University for Bible and mission training. They served in Cote d'Ivoire for fifteen years and are now in leadership at the USA headquarters of WEC International.

One couple went into the ministry, which meant leaving a prestigious job. Paul's seminary years were followed by a few years of joy in ministry, until cancer struck. Painful sacrifice and ultimately death followed, but the Wests followed the Lord lovingly and faithfully until the end. Paul's wife, Betsy, nursed him with such care that it could well have made a biblical story of sacrificial love and tenderness.

We had been at Dilworthtown Church for five years when Jim felt he was being too careful in his sermons and not challenging the congregation enough. After all we had been through in our first church, he feared upsetting the apple cart. He became convicted that his message was to be a clear call to be willing to follow the Lord anywhere, at any cost, however that might work out—including in the workplace or into mission work. He also was aware that it would not be popular to call for giving self and wealth even beyond faithful participation and tithing, which most of our congregation already practiced.

Knowing all of this, Jim determined that, at the risk of emptying the church, he would preach what God was directing. The covenant group promised Jim that they would pray faithfully while he preached what the Lord was requiring. It would mean challenging our dear people to die to their own desires, perhaps even by encouraging a child's desire to live a life of service overseas among the poor instead of seeking success in the corporate world.

Hopefully, one does not preach what he is not willing to give or do himself, so it followed that some of our own children would be among those going. Dave graduated from high school and, early the next morning, left with Teen Missions International to help build a hospital in the jungle of Papua New Guinea. Nancy went to Japan with TEAM to teach English for the summer. At the same time, Sue was deep-sea diving, as assistant instructor to her future husband, John, and Bill was at Fort Knox, in basic training with the Army Reserve.

After they all had departed, Kathy asked at supper one evening, "Mother, do you know where all your children are?" For someone who kept pretty close watch on them all as they were growing up, I had to admit that the answer was rather odd: "One's in a dugout canoe, going up the Sepik River in the wilds of Papua New Guinea; one is in the air on the way to Japan; one is under the sea somewhere, staring fish in the eye; and another is slugging away on marches and firing ranges." I was glad that God had a better view of where they all were and that I could at least see one of the five!

Mission would change the heart of anyone who ventured to be a part of it, but I never figured that it could also change the physique. Dave returned home with muscles I didn't know existed, enough mosquito-bite scars to make counting impossible, and so grown-up that I momentarily didn't recognize him as he stepped off the plane. Nancy, magnetized to attract Japanese people, came home with a kimono.

Even in Nancy's first year at college, Japanese students had felt at home with her, and they delighted that an American would help them cook and eat the national foods they sometimes prepared. As Christmas approached, one of the Japanese girls at college asked if she could accompany Nancy home for the holidays. I would be recovering from surgery, so I was hesitant to host a guest. Nancy, forgetting she would be employed over the holiday break, assured me she would take care of Noriko.

As I was welcoming them, I had my first glimpse of Christmas through the eyes of a Buddhist. Here we were, all decked out with crèches in just about every room and red candles burning. I could visualize her translating this into little gods and us burning candles to them! Horrified, I quickly explained that we did not always decorate like this, only to be assured that her family celebrated Christmas, too. Celebrated *Christmas*? I had understood she was a Buddhist. "Oh, we have Christmas tree, too." There would be a lot of explaining, with many hand motions, in the days to follow.

Nancy was at her daily job at the fish market, and poor Noriko was wilting for want of speaking her own language. At lunch one day, I served cookies cut in the shapes of the biblical Christmas figures, and she asked what they were. When I started to relate the story, I could see the disbelief in her eyes. I suddenly realized how preposterous it must sound to an unbeliever: Mary getting pregnant out of nowhere, a king in a manger, angels appearing, and Joseph just accepting it all. What a tale to beat all fairy tales!

I did a hasty retreat, retrieved our Bible story book with pictures, and began at the beginning. What followed was the Caldwell twenty-minute version of the Bible, in language so simple that a professional translator would pale. All through the story, I kept repeating, "Noriko, this is *not* just a *story*. This is *true*!" "Ah so," was always her reply.

Concluding that I had bungled things badly, I called a Japanese pastor friend. I was hoping that he could spend a few hours with Noriko, so she could talk with someone in her own language. Being close to Christmas, he was too busy, but he put me in touch with a Japanese woman who would be hosting a Bible study the following evening, for students from Japan. What a pleasant "coincidence"!

Off we went with Noriko, who promised to call Nancy when dinner and Bible study were finished, so Jim and I could pick her up. Hours later, I received a call from Nancy, who was crying. Through her tears, I heard her say, "Something *awful* has happened to Noriko." My heart sank. This girl was our guest, I had confused her no end, and now she was hurt. What could be worse? Jim and I hurried to pick her up, only to be greeted by the hostess wreathed in smiles and rushing to hug me (a most un-Japanese gesture!). This did not compute!

"Here," she said, "Noriko has a Christmas present for you." With that, Noriko stepped out of the shadows with a big smile and exclaimed in her sweet Japanese accent, "Oh, Mrs. Caldwell, tonight I *beleebed*!" I had misunderstood when Nancy really had said, "Something *awesome* has happened to Noriko." Noriko had heard the Christmas story told again that night, and several Japanese had shared that they likewise had seen angels who told them of Christ.

(I later learned that this is a not an uncommon way for Japanese to be introduced to the Lord.) Home we went, rejoicing!

Noriko's Christmas present from us was a cross on a chain. At our Christmas Eve communion service, a blond-haired family with one black-haired girl knelt together, glad that the Savior had come to earth—and particularly to our house and Noriko's heart.

Noriko returned to Japan, married a Christian man whom she met at International Christian University, and walks today with Jesus.

Mission was everywhere! Someone suggested that so many were leaving to serve the Lord that perhaps we should hang a sign on the door of the church. Instead of the proverbial "Gone fishin'," it would read "Gone mission"! We were actually sending people out faster than we were taking them into membership, and we had no idea that our own obedience would soon take *us* to another place.

Jim and I attended Urbana '87 and again sensed our own call to mission. There we rededicated ourselves to the Lord's worldwide mission enterprise.

Almost immediately came a request for me to be the counselor at Morrison Academy in Taiwan. I wouldn't go anywhere without Jim, so we sought a position for him in the same city. When none developed, we knew that door was closed. Not long after that, we were asked to consider Jim becoming the pastor of the International Church in Beijing, only to have the Tiananmen Square incident occur and that door close, too.

WEC approached us about teaching in their newly formed missionary training college in the Netherlands. It seemed the perfect match! The teaching language would be English, we were familiar with the culture, and Europe would be only eight hours away from our children, who were all on their own or in college. We felt confident that this would be our new call, Jim to teach New Testament and me to teach counseling.

But that which seems right is not always the Lord's desire. WEC determined that we would not have full missionary status because of our age. After praying, we all concluded that Holland wasn't where we were to be. In any case, we knew we were being called away from Dilworthtown. "Where, O Lord?" we asked. "We'll go anywhere in the world. Just show us where."

We were ready to sell our house, leave our belongings, and go—but where? We were ready, but God's agenda had a few more curves in the road before the turn that would lead us even closer to our Father's heart.

CHAPTER 10

"ANYWHERE" IS
TWELVE MILES

I've been thru the valley, I've been thru the fire,
I've walked thru deep water, I've bowed in the mire;
I've fought in the battle with courage all gone,
But this is the reason I always go on:
Jesus is with me—my shepherd and guide,
All that I need He is there to provide;
That makes the difference—this friend by my side,
Jesus is walking with me.[1]
—John W. Peterson

LORD, you have assigned me my portion and my cup;
*   you have made my lot secure.*
The boundary lines have fallen for me in pleasant places;
*   surely I have a delightful inheritance.*
—Psalm 16:5–6

I T WAS OBVIOUS that the Lord was not going to give us
directions in neon signs, so the arduous task of going through
the Presbyterian Church's ministerial search process was before us.
The mountain of paperwork and time involved is enough to make

anyone flinch, but Jim began to fill out the forms, and we began to ask soul-searching questions.

Did Jim feel that being a solo pastor again would give him the time or opportunities to focus on mission work, to which the Lord was clearly directing us? Churches want the pastor to be centered on them, so preaching and visitation skills are always given priority when searching to fill their pulpits. Missions and outreach skills are usually far down on their wish lists, but by this time they were high on ours.

As a culture, we American Christians really have centered on ourselves and sought comfort, hence sidelining the great commission. Yet mission is the very thing that is closest to God's heart and will accomplish growth, both spiritually and in numbers. It seems that everything else is tried, from spiritual formation to exciting programs to all kinds of different worship forms.

All of these may be somewhat beneficial in bringing vitality to a church, but they just are not what Jesus prescribed. In mission we will see the world as he sees it. It is in ministering to people that we will be drawn closer to his heart and will find the personal fulfillment all other avenues seek.

We had already become aware of some of this, for Jim's original call to ministry was "to show people in the church what Christianity is really about." Now all we had to do was to find an opportunity to do that, knowing that "Go into all the world and preach the good news" (Mark 16:15) is not truly on most church people's radar screens.

After years of working with churches, I am convinced that the person who is enthusiastically involved with missions is often seen as someone who has a favorite hobbyhorse, was born with a quirk already implanted in him, or is an adventurer of the oddest sort. We didn't answer to any of the above; we simply had been carefully led into missions by God himself and wanted others to experience what we had found.

Perhaps it would be more suitable to seek an associate pastor position, although ministers who have been solo pastors do not generally or willingly step into a secondary position. How did Jim feel about this? Would he be willing to step down to number two? His willingness to do any job well and be a good executive officer, rather than the front runner, had always been a quality in him that I had both admired and puzzled over. Didn't everyone want to shine? Weren't the sights better from the top? Wasn't the peak what everyone wanted to scale? I supposed it was, *if* you were Edmund Hillary and Everest was your goal.

However, if you were following hard after God, Jesus would be the one out in front and you would always be in a secondary position. The name of the peak would be Servanthood rather than Everest, and the sight of people's faces looking up and reaching for your hand along the way would be far more satisfying than a breathtaking view.

Jim had it right; it's far better to be in a secondary position and obey God than to desire to be at the top. He began to look for associate pastor positions in our denomination's "want ads" for pastors.

As a good way to have fellowship and share concerns, Jim was in a monthly breakfast foursome of pastors in our area. One was Dick Streeter, pastor of Paoli Presbyterian Church, a large, active church not far away. A few months prior, Jim had asked Dick to speak at a stewardship dinner at Dilworthtown Church and to lead a Session retreat. Jim had been impressed with Dick's attitude about money and giving, reaching out to people, and trusting the Lord in all things.

At one breakfast, Jim mentioned to Dick, "If an associate position opens up at Paoli Church, I'm interested." Within the following two months, both of Dick's associate pastors responded to calls to other ministries and departed, so the whole configuration of the staff at Paoli would be changing. Their annual mission budget was already at nearly half a million dollars, fifty percent of total giving, so Dick envisioned a pastor to oversee outreach and asked Jim if he would be open to filling that position.

This was exactly the answer to our prayers! Things moved quickly after that: the pastoral nominating committee approved, Jim candidated, the congregation called him to be Associate Pastor of Outreach Ministries, and we were on yet another search for a house.

We had told the Lord that we would go *anywhere* in the world, and he was moving us *twelve miles*!

∽

Unknown to us while all of this was occurring, something was growing in our lives that threatened to capsize all that God was doing. Not surprisingly, when God and his people are walking in unity, opposing forces try to undo his work. One little word can strike a crushing blow: *cancer*.

Cancer was not a word unfamiliar to me or a disease which I felt could never touch me. My mother had breast cancer that resulted in a mastectomy and, years later, radiation, chemotherapy, and finally death. I had watched it eat away at her body and, while the possibility of such a legacy was real indeed, I never felt more than a little gray cloud hovering over the landscape of my health. Like many, particularly those who have youthful energy and are very busy, I assumed such things could occur to others, but not to me—at least not now, when it was most inconvenient. Oh, yes, I went for my mammograms, but the specter of such a calamity was far-removed from my everyday thinking.

One of the benefits of having to so closely depend on the Lord in the past was that constant conversation with him was always being carried on, and listening for his voice was more than an exercise. Hence the little nagging feeling, that a medical check-up might be in order, caught my attention.

From past experience, I knew that the only way to stop that nudge was to get the bothersome check-up. Jim was surprised to find out I had made an appointment, because I always resisted going for a doctor visit unless I felt terrible.

It was always good to see my old friend, Dr. Frank Vossenberg, and the visit was going along just swimmingly until he announced that there was a palpable lump in my left breast. The foreboding had just become real. I left the office somewhat shaken, dreading the results of the tests to come. Could this be happening? Now, with Jim about to change jobs and a move on the horizon? For that matter, hang the move; could this be happening at all?

After I left the doctor's office and sat waiting for a traffic light to change, two tears rolled down my face. For just as surely as I had known that I should go to the doctor, I knew beyond a shadow of doubt what the verdict of those tests would be. Cancer and I were going to tangle, and God had let me know it.

The insurance company could have spared the test costs, because I was sure that God had let me in on events to come. However, such things always have to be done in the proper order, so after a mammogram and an ultrasound, off I went for a biopsy. The results were surprising, though a little disconcerting: the lump was benign. I was clear! I had no argument with the findings; they pleased me perfectly. But what about my certainty that I had heard God so clearly?

Perhaps I couldn't hear God as well as I thought. Perhaps I was not as close to God as I hoped. I pushed those thoughts to the back of my mind and determined to rejoice in my good fortune. That lasted until a week later, when the surgeon called to say that he had felt uneasy with the pathology results and had sent the slides to the University of Pennsylvania for study. He had just received the report that, while the cyst was indeed benign, a few cancer cells in their very early stages had been discovered elsewhere on one of the slides.

To this day I don't know which was greater, my relief that I really could hear God's leading or my fear of what the future would bring. There really is "a lot more to health than not being sick."[2] That truth would be there to hang on to later.

"With your family history, I would advise a bilateral mastec-tomy." Though I heard the words of the oncologist, I was having a hard time translating "bilateral." Didn't that mean two sides? Wasn't this cancer in the very earliest of stages, almost indiscernible? Wasn't this like destroying a house to kill a flea?

But then, this was no flea, and my family history was not in my favor. A double mastectomy it would be—and quickly, so Jim could begin his new job and I would have two arms with which to pack, move, and be somewhat normal when I would meet the people of our new church.

༄

No one is ever prepared to hear the sentence of cancer, let alone make the choice to endure such assault on one's body. I was no different. Now I wondered, "How will I cope? How will I make sense of it all?" Like others, I asked the familiar question, "Why *me*?" Already knowing the medical answer, I decided that a spiritual one would be more helpful.

Years before, I had heard Dr. Helen Roseveare speak. A missionary doctor in the Congo during the Simba rebellion in the 1960s, her story has been eloquently told in Alan Burgess's book, *Daylight Must Come.*[3] Helen had been repeatedly raped, wounded in body and soul, and her life threatened. She, like everyone else, had asked that same question. I remembered her saying that the answer was simply "Why *not* me?"

That answer put my situation into perspective, and I began a walk with God that was the deepest I had experienced to date. Without my even forming a question, a verse of Scripture would jump out to direct my thoughts. It wasn't long until I was reciting with Job, "Shall we accept good from God, and not trouble?" (Job 2:10).

2 Corinthians 1:9–11 described my situation and also gave promise of hope: "Indeed, in our hearts we felt the sentence of death. But this happened that we might not rely on ourselves but on God, who raises the dead ... On him we have set our hope that he will continue to deliver us, as you help us by your prayers."

At times, I left behind the lessons of moment-by-moment living and dissolved into a pool of worry and tears, crying like Job that my heart was fainting within me. There was the possible future of motherless children, Jim trying to juggle a new call and a family by himself, and the prospect of a disfigured body. It is to their credit that my many friends did not badger me as Job's had.

Rather, one card after another would appear with verses from Psalm 91, verses reminding me who my strength and refuge truly was, that I did not need to fear the pestilence that was stalking, that God would command his angels to guard me, and that because he loved me he would be with me in time of trouble and deliver me. There was even the promise that he would satisfy me with long life—a statement I clung to, but with shaky faith.

Eliphaz had advised Job to appeal to God and lay his cause before the Almighty (Job 5:8), because Job would be restored as he yielded to God and came to be at peace with him (Job 22:21–23). I decided that was good advice for me, too. As I settled down to accept what life had thrown me and touched again the hem of Jesus' robe, there came an assurance that cancer would not claim my life. My life was firmly in God's hands, and my days had been numbered even before I was born (Ps. 139:16). Whatever might be the means of my death, it would not take away one day that had been assigned to me. It could not shorten what already was mine, and I could not lengthen my number of days by worry or pleading. A truly uplifting thought!

This trial, then, was only a very rough spot along the way that had already been ordered and established by the One who loved me! Now it made sense, and I could pray with everything in me, "Lord, since you have chosen to reveal this cancer at a stage at which I will be spared, then you must have meaning for my life ahead. If I must go through the pain, assault, and humiliation, then grant that it all will count for something."

So, feeling much like I was walking to a guillotine, I walked into the hospital one sunny June day. I couldn't imagine how I was keeping one foot going in front of the other or how it would all turn out. As I lay on the operating table and the nurses were preparing me, my arms were spread out and strapped down. I was lying there in the position of the cross and, much to my groggy astonishment, the last words I remember thinking were, "Into your hands I commit my spirit" (Luke 23:46). What safer place is there? The peace that descended was not all because of the anesthesia.

The operation was completed, and reconstruction and recovery began. No cancer cells were found anywhere else, and neither chemotherapy nor radiation was prescribed! God truly had delivered me, for as I remembered what my mother had endured, I realized that I feared those treatments almost more than cancer itself.

I thought back to Dr. Vossenberg's statement when my diagnosis had been confirmed: "Welcome to the land of the chosen few." At the time, it seemed a strange thing to say to someone who has just been told she has cancer. He explained that only a few people ever face their mortality and, having been brought to that point, I would always fully appreciate every moment that God would allow me.

Frank had been so right! Every dawn was a new and beautiful beginning. Every day was fresh and welcome, and everything in it was appreciated and a delight. The future would always begin with each day's awakening and looking forward to whatever wonders that day might contain. There would be both good and adversity, but each day would begin with thanks that I could be there to experience it all.

With that hurdle out of the way and under control, I could begin to focus on the new calling that was before us at Paoli Church, beginning with the inevitable house hunt.

Ten days later, not fully recovered from surgery, I gingerly got dressed. After shaking my head at the reflection of my new contours, or rather the lack thereof, I was ready. Admittedly, *this* search would have two redeeming features: I had only twelve miles to travel to look for a house and a dear friend and real estate agent, Marlene, had volunteered to lead the search and drive me to see what she had located.

There were only a few houses in the area for sale, and fewer that would come close to meeting my criteria. I had privately asked the Lord for a house with five particular features: be located near the church, four bedrooms (one for my counseling office), a place for my clients to park, a big backyard for our dog to run, and be in move-in condition.

Marlene and I looked at four houses, and one after the other they were vetoed—for lack of space, location, or undesirable features. I shook my head at people's tastes in colors and the results of their do-it-yourself projects. As the day progressed, my spirits became lower and lower, and my pallor became whiter and whiter. Marlene was getting concerned, but I was determined to push on.

As we drove up to the fifth house, one not even on her list but which she had just spotted, I was concentrating on staying upright and amiable. There stood a house that looked inviting, but it was at the top of a fairly steep driveway, which I was not sure I had the energy to ascend. Gathering what little strength remained, I trudged behind Marlene. As I passed the gate to the ample backyard, I noticed an arched trellis, the entry to a tiered garden surrounded by evergreen trees.

Through the fog of wishing I could be there in the shade, I heard Marlene: "This is it. This is the one for you. I believe it will meet all your requirements." Now I loved my friend, but at that point my five criteria were far from my thinking; my main concern was reaching the front door. I would have dismissed Buckingham Palace as a contender just to get back in the car and journey home to my bed.

The house was immaculate, the decoration as I would have done, and the owners were kind beyond belief. The lack of color in my face must have alarmed them, for they urged me to sit and sip the lemonade they offered before discussing the house and its sale.

After a quick tour of my required four bedrooms and the rest of the house, I stood on the huge back porch, gazing out at the small grove of trees I had seen. I hadn't asked the Lord for such a pleasant view, but he had known what would bring delight to my heart.

He had done it again! He had given above and beyond what we ask or can imagine. He had saved this for last, as his finish to the day. I hadn't thought I could go a step farther, and here was the lesson again, just as in the hymn:

> When we have exhausted our store of endurance,
> When our strength has failed ere the day is half done,
> When we reach the end of our hoarded resources,
> Our Father's full giving has only begun.[4]
> —Annie Johnson Flint

That house near the church, which met all our desires, was bought and became our home. Many were the days when I watched birds building their nests in the eaves of the big porch, the branches of those fir trees bending under snow, roses winding up the trellis, or our Sheltie racing around the backyard. I never ceased to marvel that God knew the extras that would please us—and gave them so freely.

However, I was not the only one who needed to be certain of God's will for us to have that particular house. By then, Jim was accustomed to living in manses and, knowing that the future held tuitions and weddings, was understandably hesitant to sign for a house of our own—any house. However, there were no manses available, and even though the call to the church included a sizable loan for a down payment, we were facing a mortgage that looked formidable. I had done my part, and now it would have to be God who would somehow convince Jim that we were on the right track.

I had heard of prayer rugs, throw rugs, and area rugs, though I had yet to learn how God could use a rug to convince anyone of anything. But waiting in the Dilworthtown Church basement was a rug that would be his special sign to Jim. One of our parishioners had recently moved to a retirement village and had given the church two oriental rugs. They were parked in a storage closet off the fellowship hall, rolled up until a use could be found for them.

In going through our new house again, we realized that we would need a rug for the dining room, since the owners would be taking theirs with them. Closing costs and moving expenses would deplete our meager stash of money, and we had no idea how we could afford a rug to protect that one beautiful hardwood floor. I suggested that the people who had given the rugs to the church might allow us to use one and asked Jim to inquire. The donors' response was immediate and affirmative, though we were warned that the rugs were old and not standard sizes.

Quick measurements of the most promising rug were made and, amazingly, it seemed that it would fit! As we unrolled the rug, we noticed the Karastan label underneath, so we decided to look into having it cleaned to improve its appearance. I quickly calculated how much we could afford for the cleaning. Then I called a reputable, local oriental rug dealer and blithely gave the dimensions, type, and make of the rug. I was hardly prepared for an estimate in excess of two hundred dollars. Sputtering, I told the saleswoman that I wondered if the rug was even worth that much.

There was a long silence. Then, as if talking to a not-too-bright child, she patiently explained that this particular rug was worth *nearly four thousand dollars*! I was glad for the telephone, which didn't expose the stupid expression on my face. Needless to say, we had it cleaned.

When the rug was delivered, we watched with wonder as it was rolled out over the floor and stopped *exactly* at the opposite wall—with only a quarter inch of the fringe on the baseboard's molding! Not only were its stains gone, but it fit as if it had been custom-made for that room!

Jim, who values exactness, was now thoroughly convinced that God had chosen this particular house for us, and I held my head a little higher every time I walked through the dining room. After all, I now had a home with a very valuable oriental rug! Somehow, little events like that can make large mortgages and small bank accounts much more palatable. At the same time, they show that God cares as much for decorating dining rooms as for dressing the lilies of the field.

Our home was a pleasant place indeed, and a lot of living went on while we resided there. There were college, graduations, and four more weddings for our children. With the help of the church deacons, who arranged beautiful church receptions, and a lot of creativity on our part, we managed to have weddings that any princess would envy, each for under our limit of four thousand dollars.

Bill had already departed for Florida, where architectural opportunities were more plentiful. Kathy was situated in New Jersey, teaching in a Christian school, and Sue and her husband were living in Delaware. With Dave in college and Nancy just graduated and teaching in central Pennsylvania, it registered that the birds were leaving the nest faster than I had realized.

However, when Nancy was proposed to by a young man she had met in college, it hit like a ton of bricks. Terry, her future husband, was from Albuquerque, New Mexico. How could he contemplate taking our daughter across the country to live? It was to his great credit that we could imagine no one more likeable or suitable for our daughter. We gave not only our consent when he asked, but our blessing as well. Now I just had to figure out how to face a future without this daughter with whom I shared, shopped, laughed, and reveled in her music.

The wedding came off in style, and there were tearful goodbyes as they rode off into the sunset. Although the house was quieter and I longed to hear Nancy's music and read the notes she had often left on my pillow, I came to the conclusion that there was indeed truth in the saying, "hearts are linked by God," even if the distance was from the east coast to the Rockies.

The following year, while we were still trying to adjust, Bill and Dave both announced their engagements. Dave's wedding would be the day after his commissioning as a second lieutenant. Then Bill's would follow within two months, which left precious little time to reflect on an empty nest.

But first there was a little celebration. Jim and I, with great ceremony, hung out the American flag that May. The flag flew for two weeks, causing our neighbors and the parishioners who passed our house to wonder. One inquisitive soul finally asked why we were so patriotic. Jim and I explained that, while we love our country, the colors had been unfurled this time to celebrate the end of paying tuition for twenty years, which had seemed an eternity!

We had survived the big three Ts—tithe, taxes, and tuition—while keeping our equanimity, maintaining our good humor, and managing to stay out of debtors' prison. Along with flying the flag were repeated prayers of thanks for the faithfulness of our heavenly Father!

Funny moments followed. To be closer to friends and family, Bill and Pam decided to marry in our area. Hence, I was enlisted to help put together another wedding. With both boys having ceremonies exactly eight weeks apart, Jim and I often found that we were talking about different weddings when we thought we were discussing the same one. I lived in horror that Jim would forget to change the names in his notes and would say the wrong name during the ceremony.

Then the house was quiet—too quiet. Adjusting from controlled, happy bedlam to silence wasn't easy. However, God's work can fill voids. He was quick to show us work in the church and in our presbytery that he had lined up for us. Our work in missions was at its height: in addition to being Associate Pastor of Outreach Ministries for Paoli Church, Jim was the Global Mission Advocate for our presbytery and chaired its Mission Beyond the Presbytery Division.

After a stint as vice moderator of our presbytery, I was on its Committee of Ministry and chaired two administrative commissions. In addition to seeing clients in my private counseling practice, I served on the national board of Presbyterians for Renewal, eventually becoming its vice president. It was apparent that our days would be productively full with God's children, if not with our own. There was, however, one more encounter with wedding bells.

As Kathy watched all her brothers and sisters find their mates and get married, she began to think that even though she desired marriage and a family, perhaps God had other plans for her. While she joked about becoming the first Presbyterian nun, she was determined that there would be no marriage unless God brought her a man who was a serious Christian and had all the desired godly qualities. This was a position which Jim and I heartily endorsed, and we prayed fervently that her desires would be met.

To make Kathy's situation more palatable and fulfill a promise we had made years before, we decided that we would take Kathy to Germany to see where she had been born. If there were to be no wedding, surely money could be found for a trip.

That trip was one for the memory books, much in the manner of *Our Hearts Were Young and Gay*! We visited eight countries in twelve days, learned the locations of ATMs in major cities in Europe, marveled at alpine wildflower meadows in spring, discovered that spaghetti is not available at ten o'clock at night in Saint Mark's Square in Venice, and stood in the parking lot of the US Army hospital where Kathy had been born. We had given our daughter a memory uniquely her own.

Several summers later, Kathy took a summer job at a mission organization, where she met a missionary candidate, Steve. They fell in love and once again, *our* goal was to find the means for another wedding! Well aware that her trip to Europe had depleted the coffers, Kathy leaned over backwards to cut corners. God would have none of it, though. He was going to see that his child had the very best!

Nancy offered the use of her wedding gown, and the bridesmaids and table settings were in periwinkle blue with white daisies. A prettier combination could not have been found, and daisies, in their summer abundance, hardly break the bank. Again the deacons hosted a lovely reception in the fellowship hall and out onto the side lawn of the church. It was a lovely August day with a slight breeze, the kind of day wished for by every bride.

But goodness was piled onto goodness. Parishioners lent their summer house on Cape Cod for the honeymoon. Another parishioner owned a Rolls Royce (complete with a jar of Grey Poupon in its glove compartment) and offered to drive them to and from the ceremony. As if that weren't enough, he also chauffeured them the day before the wedding, so they could run all their errands in style. In fact, he humorously suggested that their photo, standing beside the car with its famous RR insignia showing, should be sent to all their supporters with a note, "This is what we gave up to be missionaries!"

Funny though that thought was, it was not overlooked by any of us that, rather than something being given up, it is God's goodness that is *gained* as one faithfully follows the Lord.

Now that weddings were no longer demanding my attention, another matter would soon need to be addressed. One day I was strolling comfortably through the grounds of the nearby abbey, and the next day a short walk around the grocery store was excruciatingly painful. A three inch curb suddenly seemed like a mountain to be avoided at any cost, and the climb up the stairs to our second floor could only be accomplished with a massive effort and a good pull on the handrail.

I was too young to be falling apart, but something needed repair, and quickly. "Cut off at the knees" had been only an expression up to that point in my life, but those words were about to become more than just a saying. The orthopedic surgeon's remedy was just that, to cut me off at the knees and replace them!

Well, here we were again—another hospitalization and the growing realization that I was fast becoming a candidate for poster girl for the bionic woman. The dreaded surgery was scheduled, the feat was accomplished, and the long recovery began. I had been through a lot, but nothing had prepared me for the pain of this surgery or learning to walk again. Over and over, as I drifted off to sleep in the hospital, with no idea how I would manage, I would softly sing the words of a hymn:

> As a mother stills her child,
> Thou can hush the ocean wild;
>> Boisterous waves obey thy will
>> When Thou say'st to them, "Be still!"
> Wondrous Sovereign of the sea,
> Jesus, Savior, pilot me.
>> —Edward Hopper,
>> "Jesus, Savior, Pilot Me"

It was not my intention to increase the hymn repertoire of the woman in the next bed, but she would have had to be brain-dead not to have memorized the words she heard so many times!

Jesus did hush the waves of pain that rolled over me. He piloted me over the rocky way of learning to walk, charting every healing moment. When I complained to the nurse that surely nothing should take this long to heal, she reminded me that I had been cut, sawed, drilled, glued, hammered, sewed, and stapled. And when even a slight movement engulfed me in pain, I could sit on our sofa and look out at the porch and the beautiful view that God had prepared for me, many years before.

Learning to walk all over again was a new kind of challenge. However, this time it was done with the adult knowledge of what it takes to accomplish the task: courage, persistence, and dependence on another. Just as I could lean on Jim when I began my shaky attempts at putting one foot in front of the other, so could I lean on Jesus as my shepherd and guide. The pain eventually diminished and my steps became firmer, but my conviction never faded that this was just another step in the journey to the heart of God.

Thus it was with thankfulness that time spent on our sofa allowed for a great deal of refection on other things as well, especially the fantastic experiences we had had on mission fields, insights we had gained along the way, the great expanses of God's kingdom we had seen, friendships with his people all over the world, and opportunities to be used by him in the healing of the hurting souls he had sent to me for counseling.

Ah, this was truly a journey one wouldn't want to miss! There were aspects that I would not choose to repeat, but none of it had been wasted. I found myself asking once again, "Why *me* ?" However, this time I did not mean "why did it *happen* to me," but rather "why had he let me *see* so much and have a glimpse into his great heart?"

CHAPTER 11

MISSIONS AND MIRACLES

We've a story to tell to the nations
That shall turn their hearts to the right,
A story of truth and mercy,
A story of peace and light.

We've a Savior to show to the nations
Who the path of sorrow hath trod,
That all of the world's great peoples
Might come to the truth of God.
—H. Ernest Nichol

***Therefore go and make disciples of all nations,
baptizing them in the name of the Father and of
the Son and of the Holy Spirit, and teaching them
everything I have commanded you. And surely I am
with you always, to the very end of the age.***
—Matthew 28:19–20

A PASTOR'S WIFE is certain to spend hours after services
waiting for her husband to finish talking to people and tie
up loose ends, and I was no exception. I counted the floor tiles,

straightened the tracts in the literature rack, read the left-behind bulletins twice, and caught up on all of the missionaries' letters while I patiently (or not too patiently) waited for Jim to exit.

The large stained glass window in the narthex, which portrayed Jesus washing his disciples' feet, was repeatedly noted during those irritating waits. Likewise, the missionary pictures in the cloister were reviewed, the maps memorized, the names rehearsed, and those missionaries prayed for, again and again.

As I waited—and waited—these pieces came together. They were people who were doing what the Lord had been doing, ministering to those who had accumulated the dust and weariness of the world. Those missionaries were the ones up close, seeing the world's needs through his eyes and ministering in his name.

Missions, it seemed, was a main window into God's heart. We might experience how great God is and see his provision and faithfulness in our own lives, but the magnitude of his heart and love could only be learned among his people in the many places they live and in their varied circumstances. It was no wonder, then, that Jesus had told us to go into *all* the world.

Imagining just wasn't going to do it. We would have to see, touch, smell, feel, and "walk a mile in their moccasins." So began our venture into the wonderful, exciting, challenging, and sometimes disturbing ministry of taking our parishioners on mission trips.

To be quite honest, we weren't sure how to start, but looking more assured than we felt, and having learned some of the lessons of God's guidance and provision in our own past, Jim and I began. Our goals were to provide experiences that would let others discover those same insights and to bless those we would visit.

If ever we were glad that we were not cut out of the same material, it was now. Jim's attention to detail, which more than once had frustrated me, could be relied upon to assure that publicity and applications were accomplished, required shots were obtained, travel arrangements were correct and secured, proper contacts were made, visas and passports were in order, and the itinerary and back-up support were in place.

My creative ideas, which had often caused Jim to shake his head and mutter, were now welcomed. Suggestions and ideas were needed for where to go, what experiences would benefit our people most, and ministry to do on the field. Training in puppetry, mime, and clowning was needed for those who had never attempted anything so out-of-character.

Jim's methodical approach and my daring made the right combination, and together we would share an array of experiences that would eventually cause others to seek our expertise—and would lead to the ministry we would share in retirement.

Mexico seemed a good place to begin our trip experiences. It was not too far away, some of our people could speak a smattering of Spanish, and we had a good missionary connection there. Humorously, we reasoned that at least it was attached by land and, if all went awry, there was the possibility we could walk home!

This would be our introduction to miming, clowning, and a whole lot more. There were fifteen on our team. We would be working with some churches in the outlying sprawl of Mexico City, ministering to street children. Then we were to join some Mexican Christians for four days in the mountains, to work on a future group home for those homeless children.

We had been told that we would have a trailer with cooking facilities at our mountain location, so in my mind I viewed a stove, running water, and electricity. I didn't expect state-of-the-art equipment, but upon entering the trailer I immediately went into a combination of denial, disbelief, and shock.

I was in charge of feeding the team, and staring at me was a gas stove with only one working burner. The "running water" would be either the result of my running to and from the artesian well a half mile away or pouring from the ladle I spotted in the vat of dubious water in the corner. The light was a stack of candles and sufficient matches to blow us sky-high if they ever connected with the gas!

However, leaders must appear confident and in control, so I tried to look nonplussed. I put on a smile, valiantly took charge, laid out on the bed nearby (the one without a mattress) all the food supplies we had brought with us, and managed to look fearsome! Anyone in my path would be sure to notice, and Jim was the first to do that.

It was pouring rain. We were in an area that had been volcanic, so, as the rain continued, the dusty ground became a kind of cement that stuck to shoe soles. Step by step the soles got thicker and thicker, and the owner of the shoes became taller and taller. Jim, taller by two inches, stopped by the trailer to cheerfully tell me that dinner would need to be soon. In he came, cement and all, the "all" being a stray cat. Pussy proceeded to make herself at home on the warm stove, cement paws just short of my one burner.

Soon? Cheerful? Did the man have no sense or reason? And worse, he had forgotten (or at least was wise enough not to mention) that this was our wedding anniversary! The cat was hastily dispatched, thrown out into the rain and cement. Had Jim not been those two inches taller, he might have followed in the same manner!

In the far recesses of my sanity, I could hear words like patience, long-suffering, gentleness, kindness, and a list of other virtues. If Satan were trying to undermine a budding mission career, he was off to a good start. Putting on the whole armor of God, I set about to do battle with the elements and anything else that would be thrown at me, and thrown at me it was!

The altitude was 7,000 feet, at which water did not boil hot enough to cook spaghetti quickly. An hour and a half later, when the soggy feast was served, the smiles and ravings of the starved team did a lot to soften what would be the cumbersome cleanup process. By the light of a candle, kept upright by its own wax, we waited another hour for water to boil, so we could wash the dishes and rinse them with our "running water."

Weary, I made my way through the rain and cement to the outhouse and then back to the trailer and welcome sleep, giving thanks that "tomorrow is another day" and shifting so my blanket was not under the leak in the roof.

Somewhat rested, I was up early and relaxed, knowing that our Mexican friends would soon come and take over the cooking.

As promised, they arrived with large smiles, much hugging, and proclamations that "everything we have is yours." Things were looking up, and I heaved a sigh of relief.

Determined that I would look at this whole experience as "virtue training," I decided to go to town to buy tomatoes. Before leaving, however, I paused and, moved by some unknown impulse, put six eggs under a blanket in the closet at the back of the trailer. As the pickup truck bounced and careened over the four miles of ruts and bumps into town, I silently wondered if all this might have been too much for me. Had I had completely lost my grip on reality? After all, eggs didn't need to incubate before they were used.

The trip was delightful. We bought our tomatoes, saw a bit of the lovely mountain countryside, and managed not to get lost. We arrived back in good spirits, greatly anticipating the noonday meal.

What a feast our friends had laid out! I marveled at the amount of food and wondered where it had all come from, for surely they had not brought it all with them. *Oh, no!* I quietly excused myself from the outdoor table and looked inside the trailer. It couldn't be! All the food that had been sitting on that bunk bed, to make meals for our remaining days there, had been turned into this one delicious feast!

It had *all* been used except some cooking oil and the Bisquick, which probably had been spared because the directions were in English. All of the lemonade packets had been made into lemonade, using up more than half of our precious bottled drinking water, and hordes of flies were loving every sip of it!!

As I stared out the door at the team, I hoped they were enjoying their last meal. Ah yes, everything our Mexican sisters had was ours and, without our even offering, what was ours had just become theirs! Actually a nice arrangement, if you can keep the spiritual lesson in mind!

Concluding that the best way to deal with this was to simply accept that anything could happen on a mission trip, I decided to cool off and bathe at the local artesian well. It would be good to be clean again and to see actual running water. Grabbing a towel, off I marched.

Sharing the well's cistern with a few men shaving, as well as with women doing their laundry and washing dishes, hadn't been counted on. But this was just something more to be accepted, so I jumped in, fully clothed. Surprisingly, I rather enjoyed the whole experience.

While my clothes dried on the long walk back, I mused that either I was made of better stuff than I had recently demonstrated or I was beginning to enter into their culture—with more joy than I thought possible. After all, they had welcomed me to join them with cheerful smiles and made space for me upstream from the laundry and barbering!

Arriving back at the trailer, I found our Mexican friends in a tizzy, packing up to leave. Their bus had developed a leaky tire, and they would have to leave immediately if they were to reach home before the tire went flat. The last woman to board the bus pointed me to a pile of cactus, which she had just picked for dinner. As I wished them well and waved, off they rode.

There was only one problem: I had never cooked cactus, and Betty Crocker was nowhere to be found! Oh well; when in doubt, shrug and don't forget to take off the spines. Yes, we had cactus, fried in our remaining oil. To my amazement, everyone proclaimed that dinner was delicious!

It seemed I was getting good at survival skills, so now all I had to do was to figure out what tomorrow's meal would be. What was that passage about feeding the five thousand? Surely Jesus could feed this mere handful. I went to sleep asking for his grace and a good idea for the morning menu, as well as suggesting to him that manna would be acceptable.

Ah yes, the Bisquick. Now a few eggs were all I needed. *Eggs?* I asked my fellow cook, Sue, to go look under the blanket in the closet. She looked at me as though I were fried without the benefit of being an egg. There, lying in state, were the six eggs I had hidden! The resulting pancakes were eaten without anyone knowing of our depleted larder.

Now that I was sure Jesus was in charge and I didn't have to worry, I went on a treasure hunt. A wonderful verse in Isaiah promises "treasures of darkness, riches stored in secret places"

(Isa. 45:3), and so there were. Under the bed and in that dark closet, we turned up a few cans of baked beans, peaches, and odds and ends—a strange assortment to prayerfully stretch for our remaining meals. We made it through with just enough and nothing to spare, discovering that when safe drinking water is gone, soda and toothpaste make a unique, sudsy combination when brushing teeth!

Before surmising that this was an inauspicious way to begin our mission work, let me remind you that experience writes a book. By the time we headed home, I had the substance of what would become the twenty-four-page team handbook for all of our church's future mission trips, as well as for churches where we would lead mission workshops in our retirement.

There were also poignant experiences that touched our souls and cannot adequately be put into words. How could we digest the sorrow of a mother in the bus terminal begging us to take her child to the USA, so she would have a better life? How does one ever forget turning her away, as she pled and wept? Or would we ever cease wondering what became of the street children, who emerged from the sewers at night to look for food in trash bins? Was the sight of a woman begging in the square, in the shadow of the great cathedral of Mexico City, the same picture our Lord sees? How much more did God want us to see of his children, and why did we think that our two weeks would make a difference?

Amid tears, our "main line" women asked that very question after our first visit to the streets at night, and there was only the answer that Jesus had given: "whatever you did for one of the least of these brothers of mine, you did for me" (Matt. 25:40). He hadn't said for how long, only that we would do it at all—that we would care enough, for even a little while, to ease the pain that broke their hearts and his.

We saw this repeated over and over, but perhaps nowhere as vividly as in India. Women were cutting grass with scissors to glean enough to sell so they could buy food for their families. A boy repeatedly jumped through a fiery hoop held by his mother, his hair catching on fire, all for a few rupees. There came the awareness that we could not be his salvation—nor, for that matter, salvation for any of the others.

However, we did have something to give: the gift of the message of Jesus' love and redemption. That truth was made very clear the morning I sat in an English-speaking church in Tamil Nadu, South India. The service had not started on time, for many of the members had walked for miles in sandals, barefooted, or on crutches.

I was in the front pew so, as they knelt to receive communion, I had a good look at their callused, dusty feet before me. I turned to watch others coming forward, with smiles and joy on their faces, singing "Count Your Blessings." Utterly dumbfounded, I asked, "Lord, what do they have to count?" His answer: "They have me."

Touring Durbar Square in Patan, Nepal, we viewed the Buddhist temples which no one has entered in the centuries since they were built. They contain idols of the gods that rule the lives of those who worship them in fear of their displeasure.

In the huge, sprawling Hindu temple in Madurai, South India, we witnessed obeisance to a live elephant—manacled and bespangled. We wondered how the pilgrims could miss seeing who was more powerful, this "god" or the man who could manacle him.

At the towering bronze Buddha in Kamakura, Japan, we watched those coming to pray, clapping their hands to try to catch his attention. We wished they could know the Savior who never slumbers nor sleeps, who is always awake to their needs. We marveled at the plentiful technology of that land, the fast bullet trains, the order, the pristine parks tended and pruned to perfection. And we sadly realized that such plenty will continue to hide what they are missing. Where are those who are willing to give themselves to share the good tidings of the God who requires not performance, but simple trust in his love and forgiveness?

Among the Punjabis in Birmingham, England, I sipped tea and studied the Bible with women who had to sneak out of their houses to avoid being beaten by their non-believing husbands. We heard testimonies from Christians in Turkey who had been imprisoned, beaten, and left for dead.

Every experience deepened our realization that the cost, time, and energy of a few mission trips was our admission to the deeper chambers of God's compassionate and caring heart.

As our hearts were being broken by the things that break the heart of God, and as we were beginning to understand the scope and importance of the task Jesus had left us, there were also pleasant lessons and interventions of God, better known as the miracles of missions.

Scripture was coming alive in every way and in every country. Yes, the feeding of the five thousand was real; hadn't he just fed a small mission team? Yes, treasure is in darkness; hadn't we found much needed food? If you go fishing, and the first fish you see has the needed coin in its mouth, that's not much different from finding baked beans under a bed when you needed them.

Looking up to the hills, thinking "where does my help come from?" (Ps. 121:1) takes on a whole new meaning when you are on the back of a camel, winding your way up Mt. Sinai at two o'clock in the morning. With a several-hundred-foot drop to your right, an equally steep drop on your left, a camel driver who speaks no English, and a camel who pauses to peer into those black ravines, up is a good direction to look—to God, who calms the fearful heart!

Standing in the temple in Karnak, Egypt, where a short distance away are ages-old homes of biblical times, built of mud bricks with straw still visible, it is easy to picture the Hebrews stomping in the mud pits to make them. Hieroglyphics inscribed on a stone wall of the temple, a record of the battle described in 1 Kings 14:25–26, make the biblical account real.

While watching elephants, lions, zebras, and wildebeests roaming the Masai Mara in Kenya, cheetahs racing across the plains, hippos bellowing their calls as they wade in the river, giraffes contentedly munching on acacia trees, and antelopes leaping for the joy of running, creation and Eden are not far from the mind's eye. But there were other reminders of that garden where sin had entered: the kill lying in the grass by the road and the Ivorian congregation of two hundred, of which only ten had jobs because they are Christians and therefore denied work by Muslim employers. Hatred is strong, and humans as well as animals still devour each other.

Truly, we had seats on the fifty-yard line. We were not only learning lessons and seeing the truths of Scripture, but we were also seeing the larger world as it really is—much more than the beautiful, sparkling land of plenty that is our normal habitat. It crossed our minds that we had been given one of the greatest privileges that human beings can experience; we really had begun to see the world as God sees it.

More than cautious about health procedures, our track record of getting people to the field and safely home in good condition was sterling. However, any winning streak sees its end eventually, and we were not to escape without a downturn.

Water in India leaves a lot to be desired in purity. When a young woman on our team nicked her leg, it didn't occur to her that bathing would cause a problem. Why would it? After all, the water was coming out of a faucet and appeared clean, and isn't all water at least safe to bathe in? She began to be short of breath, her temperature rose, and her leg turned a startling shade of pink—all signs, even to the non-medical eye, that something was truly amiss.

Our team attended a dinner that evening, at the New Delhi YMCA where we were staying, with the Presbyterian Church (USA)'s representative in India and the directors of medicine and nursing for the Church of North India. Much to our surprise and pleasure, Dr. Beverly Booth, a well known epidemiologist and the only American doctor in Delhi at the time, had also been invited. I had heard of her, as one of the outstanding graduates of the college I had attended.

At dinner, I mentioned that we would be going on to Nepal to meet another missionary, also a graduate of our alma mater. Wouldn't it be nice for me to write, for the Beaver College magazine, about the three of us meeting on the other side of the world? Beverly gave me her card, which I casually put in my pocket.

Later that evening, our team member's leg had turned from pink to red, and I realized that we were about to have a medical catastrophe on our hands. Jim and I were in a quandary about how to find any suitable help. This was a place where bacteria and lack of medicines seemed to make health care a fairy tale, not the inalienable right that Americans are led to believe it is. And if the water in India leaves a lot to be desired, hospitals leave even more so, for the patient's family is expected to provide all meals and non-medical care.

As we prayed, my nose started to run, so I put my hand in my pocket to retrieve a Kleenex and came up with Beverly's card. I forgot my runny nose and made a hasty exit to find a phone. Beverly was home! She spoke English! She was a doctor! She was a lifesaver! She was God's miracle!

Beverly not only made a "house call" and saw to the needed medical care, but she took our teammate into her own home. With all the intravenous tubes and paraphernalia needed for treatment, she was doctor, host, cheerleader, and comforter.

Some might like to call that unlikely set of events "fortuitous circumstances," but "miracle" seems to fit better. Let's enumerate those circumstances: Dr. Booth was the only American doctor in

Delhi at the time, as well as a PCUSA mission worker; an invitation extended that had not been planned; fellow alumnae meeting across the ocean; the event occurring the evening we realized that medical intervention was needed; a business card slipped into a pocket, to surface when needed; and a nose that needed attention at the crucial time. Only One with the wisdom and power to make it happen could have arranged all that—especially the nose part!

Many had heard stories of the struggling church in Russia, so it was exciting when a Russian pastor, who was visiting the United States right after *glasnost*, was asked to speak at our Paoli Church's Christmas Eve service. His story was compelling. In the course of his sharing, he mentioned that to build a church in Russia right then would cost only ten thousand dollars!

Before the offering was taken, Pastor Dick Streeter, whose "hunches" often turned out to be the Lord's whisper, announced to the congregation that Paoli Church was going to do just that—build a church in Russia. Both Jim and I were a bit stunned. Christmas gifts were one thing, but this Russian pastor had not been talking about a few sets of Lincoln Logs.

Usually the Christmas Eve offering was around five thousand dollars and was allotted for a specific purpose, but Dick covered that too. The first five thousand dollars of the offering would go for its designated purpose, but everything over that would be the beginnings of a Russian church.

The service concluded with the usual "Silent Night," sung in the soft light of six hundred candles, flickering and casting their glow around the sanctuary. The worshippers made their way out with the cheerful greetings that always accompany that evening. The offering was secured in the safe until it could be counted after Christmas.

A few days later, when the counters finished and announced the total, it was fourteen thousand nine hundred seventy-five dollars!—enough for the usual Christmas commitment *plus* all except twenty-five of the ten thousand dollars needed for a Russian church building. Dick was elated, we were walking on air, and the counters were almost in shock. As Dick returned to his office, he noticed that a check had been slid under his door. It had been put there by someone who had not been able to put it in the plate. The amount? Twenty five dollars!

Now, I am more curious about how God arranges things like this than about how Jesus turned water into wine, and I have every intention of asking when we have one of our long talks in eternity. But this I know now: that amazing Christmas Eve offering was the beginning of a long, close, and thrilling relationship with Russian Baptists.

It would result in our taking a team to Russia, seeing that church outgrow the building we had enabled them to build, helping other Russian churches, and establishing a warm relationship with the president of the new Moscow Theological Seminary. In later years, we would help two Presbyterian congregations form sister-church partnerships with Russian congregations.

Sweet and touching moments with the Russians were many, like the time we were worshiping in a church in Lipetsk and the pastor's wife rose and sang a hymn. While we could not understand the words, we recognized it as "Beyond the Sunset." I felt the gentle hand of God nudging me to join her. As she concluded, I stood beside her and we sang the hymn again together, in our two languages, and watched as tears filled the eyes of Christians who had not been able to share their faith with those from abroad for seventy years.

There was the time Jim stood in the Kremlin and saw two Russian soldiers also enjoying the sights of that magnificent place. Jim had been an army officer in Germany when the Berlin Wall was erected, and there had been many moments when it seemed certain that war would erupt. Never in his wildest dreams had he imagined visiting Russia, nor had he ever thought that he might speak to or relate in any way to the "enemy," even in a military capacity. Jim walked over to the soldiers and, with the help of our interpreter, told them he had been a lieutenant in the American

Army in Germany. I remember the tears in his eyes as he shook hands with them.

That experience led to another memorable one. We had been asked to speak to a church that met in a movie theater. We were on the stage with no pulpit, the choir behind us, and a sound system that mirrored the dysfunctional conditions of a country just free of the Communist regime.

Before each service, Jim and I usually compared notes as to what we would be saying, but there had been no time for such coordination this particular evening. I had been asked to sing and Jim to give the sermon. I most often began with a brief explanation of the song and a Scripture verse or two.

I rose to sing and began as usual, only to notice the horror-stricken look on Jim's face. I had used the Scripture with which he had planned to begin his sermon! Out of the corner of my eye, I could see him furiously thumbing through his Bible, looking for a new text. Oh, we were off to a great beginning!

At the moment I finished speaking, there was a colossal bang behind me. A quick glance revealed that someone had fallen off the bleachers, so one less choir member would be singing. There was nothing to do but plunge ahead. I began to sing. There was silence, then a crackle, then a sputter, then another crackle; the microphone was singing its own song. What to do but sing louder than the sound system?

Just as I was wondering what more could possibly happen, in through the back door ran a little white dog, who had decided he wanted to go to church that evening. He announced his entrance by punctuating my song with sharp little yips. The best that could be said for all of the distractions was that Jim recovered his equilibrium, and a valuable lesson was learned. Ever since, we have always managed to check with each other before ministering together.

While God was chuckling at the unfolding events, he had worked his purposes. In the congregation were many men about our age, who had served in the Soviet Army. The sermon Jim had so quickly rearranged ended with a message of reconciliation like none I have since experienced.

Jim shared that he had ridden along the East German border with Russians standing opposite, ready with automatic rifles. He told of the huge red sign facing west, declaring in bold white German words, "*Socialism will triumph.*" He related the experience of shaking hands with those Russian soldiers in the Kremlin, and then he spoke words that we all need to hear: "Socialism has not triumphed. Capitalism will not triumph, either. Only Jesus Christ will triumph!"

I witnessed the tears of grown men who knew and heard again that wonderful truth. For a moment, I could believe that peace on earth was a possibility.

Years later, when 9/11 happened while we were again in Russia, we experienced their compassion and concern for Americans. Russians placed flowers, candles, and flags of both countries in front of the U.S. Embassy, and their soldiers were standing guard at its doors. We were told that the entire student body of Moscow Seminary had been in prayer for the United States and for us. Most touching was the offer that, should our return home be delayed, we could live in the seminary president's dacha.

In those precious times, we truly experienced what Jesus had prayed, "that all of them may be one" (John 17:21). Those were moments that made our hearts sing in concert with the angels and in time with the beating of God's heart.

It was a *big* flag—one by two meters, to be exact.

Jim had just accepted that gift of thanks from the Presbyterian Church (USA)'s first missionaries to Kazakhstan. Paoli Church had given $17,000 to enable them to go and serve there, and they had just presented the church with that country's flag. I could well imagine Jim's thoughts, as he held it up for all to see. Where could it be hung? Where was a place big enough for it?

Even if we had tried, we could never have imagined what God had in mind for the part that flag would play. Jim soon folded the flag and stored it away for safekeeping, never forgetting it, but never finding a use for it. Why would we suspect that it would become the key to one of our most remarkable mission stories, of how God can use anything to bring sheep into his fold.

Two years later, we were on our way to Kazakhstan to assist another missionary, a son of a family in our church. Matt worked with a lovely Russian young woman, helping children in state-run orphanages. We knew of his plan to become engaged to her while we were visiting.

To add a special touch, we decided to bring, in addition to our materials for working with the children, enough decorations, goodies, and presents to give the young couple a wedding shower. It would be both a surprise and something out of the ordinary, for bridal showers are not part of Russian culture. Somehow, along with the dental equipment we were also taking, we stuffed our suitcases with crepe paper streamers and wedding bells, housewares, negligees, and fancy paper plates. We just hoped that we would not raise too many eyebrows when we went through customs.

Matt proposed. Anna accepted. The entire family attended the shower, which resembled a fairy tale unfolding, with the eleven mission team members standing in for Flora, Fauna, and Merriweather. Seeing Anna warmly embraced and honored by us, her parents were so moved that her father offered to be our team's guide while we were in the area.

Neither of Anna's parents was a Christian. Although her mother had shown some interest in Christianity, her father, while polite toward us about the concept, was not at all enamored. He had been a member of the party and was a well-educated man, a lawyer with all the arguments against Christianity of anyone who had grown up and lived under that atheistic regime.

At a former Soviet army camp in the mountains, we met more than a hundred orphans, whom members of our church had sponsored for a three-day vacation. We sang, shared biblical stories through puppets, talked, fell in love with all of them, and were soundly beaten by them at ping pong. Our team dentist checked and fixed all of their teeth, and one of our team, an algebra and geometry teacher, quickly learned the fine points of being a dental assistant.

It was a special time, in a beautiful setting in the mountains, which ended in an even more beautiful service of baptism. Forty-eight children who had accepted the Lord asked to be baptized. As one of the last children professed his faith in the waist-deep water of the rocky swimming pool, their housemother shyly asked to join them, in baptism and in the kingdom of God.

Upon our return to the city, Anna's father, Victor, escorted us around that beautiful metropolis. Our team took in the sights of the old wood church, the market, and the war memorial. We looked down the street that had once been the Silk Road, the artery for caravans coming from the East. Victor also accompanied us to the mountains, where we experienced the charm of eating in a yurt and enjoyed the spectacular views across the valley, to the snow-covered peaks.

After our mountain-top experience, Victor had more in store for us. With his usual graciousness, he announced that he would host our last evening meal in Kazakhstan.

In the restaurant, enjoying Kazakh specialties, we answered Victor's question about what we had enjoyed most about our trip. After we shared, it seemed only right to ask what had impacted him about us. That could have been awkward to answer, so we relaxed when he responded that what impressed him most was that we would pay to travel such a distance just to help these children.

Then, to everyone's surprise, he announced that now, knowing our concern for his people, he had changed his mind; he and his wife would travel to the United States for his daughter's wedding ceremony there. Until then he had declined to come, saying that the civil ceremony in his own country would be enough. Matt and Anna were overjoyed.

During our flight home, our thoughts were on how we could welcome our new friends to our country when they arrived a few months later. How could we make their visit just as special as Victor had made ours?

The big day arrived. A Russian pastor had been invited to attend both the ceremony and the reception to translate for Tanya and Victor. While the church was being prepared, Jim remembered that huge Kazakhstan flag on a shelf in his office closet. It seemed just the finishing touch to place it in the chancel with the United States and Christian flags.

And so it was, when Victor entered a Christian church for the first time in his life, that he was welcomed by both the Spirit of Jesus Christ and a symbol of his homeland. We learned later that it was the presence of his country's flag that began the softening of Victor's heart.

A reception followed at Matt's parents' home. Jim and I were seated with Tanya, Victor, and the friendly Russian pastor, Sasha, who launched into animated conversation in their native language. Jim and I, understanding no more than an occasional "nyet" or "da," gained a deeper appreciation of Paul's admonition about the need for interpretation when speaking in tongues. From the smiles and headshaking, however, we surmised that all was well.

We didn't have to wait long until our assumptions were verified. Sasha asked me to gather a few women and pray with Tanya, for she had just expressed a desire to accept Jesus Christ as her Savior. There was more than one union completed that day—the union of a happy couple and the union of a Russian mother and her Lord for eternity. Victor accepted the events that had just unfolded but declined to follow his wife's action, as this was so new to him.

Matt and Anna returned to Kazakhstan and their work there, and soon we rejoiced to hear that Anna's brother and grandfather also had come to Christ. God's salvation had, indeed, come to their household, but we wondered if and how that would ever include Victor. Truly, what God begins, he finishes well, and often with a flourish. A few years later, we heard that Victor, too, had walked into the kingdom of God—and straight into seminary!

A journey to Kazakhstan, a wedding shower, ministry to orphans, and sharing our lives all might have parts in paving a road that leads to eternity. But a flag?

I often think of how many more stories we will see finished, how many more people whom we never dreamed we had touched will share God's glory with us in eternity, and how many more "insignificant" things he will have used to enlarge his family. It makes the excitement of sports events puny by comparison and the sharing of the gospel one of the most compelling, exciting endeavors imaginable. Indeed, at the unfolding of important events of this age, we have had front row seats!

While the stories and miracles kept us enthralled, what we had seen emphasized how much remains to be done for the Master. That need would propel us into our retirement years with a renewed commitment to continue on in the service of our King. There is always another chapter ahead in the story we have to tell to the nations.

CHAPTER 12

HEALING HEARTS

Down in the human heart, crushed by the tempter,
    Feelings lie buried that grace can restore;
Touched by a loving heart, wakened by kindness,
    Cords that are broken will vibrate once more.
Rescue the perishing, care for the dying;
    Jesus is merciful, Jesus will save.
           —Fanny J. Crosby,
             "Rescue the Perishing"

*Let us hold unswervingly to the hope we profess,
for he who promised is faithful. And let us consider
how we may spur one another on toward love and
good deeds.*
                    —Hebrews 10:23–24

CONSIDERING THE GENERATIONS of teachers in my family and my parents' emphasis on thinking of others, it's not a stretch to see how I would become involved in a teaching career and missions. Not even in sight was how I would eventually have a counseling practice for more than twenty-five years.

Not having even the remotest desire to pursue that profession, majoring in psychology in addition to elementary education had been merely an expedient choice, calculated to qualify me for admission to medical school. I had pored over Dad's *Gray's Anatomy*, studying the illustrations and trying to make sense out of the Latin names. The dream of being a doctor was always foremost, for helping to heal people was the best profession imaginable.

There was only one real problem, as I saw it. Looming large was the lack of enthusiasm for acceptance of women into the medical profession in those days. Dr. Ann Gray Taylor, the obstetrician who had cared for my mother, cheered me on. However, Dad and Mom were not open to sending their daughter to medical school and then have her marry a doctor and never practice medicine.

Mom and Dad brought up a few more problems. There were the four of us to be educated and not a preponderance of money. Would it be fair of me to use more than my share, especially when my talent for teaching had already been proved?

During summers while in junior high, I accompanied Mom to her teaching job in a preschool and often substituted for teachers who were absent. I had tutored in reading and history since seventh grade, taught afternoon classes in chemistry for high school football players, and managed a township summer playground program. In my thinking, I had *already* had a career in teaching and wanted to move on to accomplish my medical desires. Mom and Dad were immovable.

To jump the hurdle of the money it would take, my goal was to get a full-tuition scholarship. After all, how could they argue the cost if they weren't paying it? I got the scholarship, to nearby Beaver College. In my parents' favor, they were not unreasonable; they agreed that as long as my major was elementary education, I could also take any additional courses.

In that era, if a student there remained on the dean's list, she could add any additional courses at no cost. The college obviously thought any such student would be reasonable enough not to take an unwieldy load. Little did they count on my determination, and so began semesters of my carrying eighteen to twenty-two credits.

How I lit upon psychology as an area of study was simple: psychology courses were the only ones that would fit with my education major and qualify me for medical school. And so it was settled. Now all I had to do was learn to spell "psychology" and stay on the dean's list! I did both.

～

It simply never entered my head that God had his own preferences for how I was to proceed. Unknown to me, his hand was already moving.

If I picture God rearranging the pieces of life, it includes him skillfully placing the pieces called "Jim" and "love" into the puzzle in my senior year. I decided that the M.D. after my name could wait for a while, in favor of a Mrs. in front of it. We were married and left for Germany while Jim served in the Army. This doctor project was going to take longer than hoped.

After settling in and getting acclimated to the cultural changes, I began to explore. Not too far from our home in Nürnberg was the University of Erlangen, which had an excellent medical school! I could hardly wait to tell Jim, who was riding around the countryside on a maneuver and would be home in a few weeks. That he would not be overjoyed at my discovery was not even a remote consideration.

When Jim came home, I broached the subject over a hearty meal with all the hope I could muster. Had the expense and our second lieutenant's monthly salary of $223.30 been considered, I might have been more hesitant. However, it was not the money to which Jim objected; it was coming home to more of a student than a wife after weeks of border duty.

Did it matter *that* much? One look at Jim and I knew it most certainly did and had to admit that, had the shoes been reversed, my feeling would have been the same. Oh, bother! Once again, my dream went back on the shelf.

The void was filled by teaching kindergarten at the American Military School in Nürnberg. That kept me busy until I began to feel strangely ill every morning. The illness was a rather common malady, remedied by the birth of a child nine months later. Life was getting full indeed.

Occasionally, during two o'clock morning feedings, I wondered how or if my dream would ever come to fruition and sometimes thought that God had neither heard my prayers nor cared. Just assuming that my plans were his, it didn't occur to me that I hadn't even asked his opinion. There was always tomorrow. Somehow, someway, someday *maybe* it would all happen. Maybe.

Jim and the Army parted, we returned to civilian life in the USA, and then began the parade of babies that would eventually fill our home with five children and the love and events that keep a family occupied. With each successive child, however, it became startlingly clear that my medical dream was fading farther into the background. After shedding more than a few hot tears, the dream was filed under the title "not to be," and I set myself to totally being the wife and mother I had become. After all, when five college educations were looming in the future, there was no possibility of pursuing my own any further.

The door was closed and would remain so. In my busyness, I didn't even look for the window that God is said to open when a door closes. That should have been the end of the story, but some dreams take time, and God had his own plan for my life.

Years later, when Jim went to seminary and the need arose for me to supply the family income, that teaching degree that Mom and Dad had insisted upon was waiting to be used. Not only did teaching supply the money needed, but having the same schedule as our children kept us together as a family.

In my more contemplative moments, I concluded that God had honored my keeping his commandments to obey my parents and cherish my husband. Could it be that God's direction for my life had been better than my own?

❧

Psychology and I had long since parted ways, unless the psychology used in child-rearing could be counted. My days were filled with papers to be graded and with teaching and nurturing children, others' as well as mine. There was precious little time for anything else, and certainly none for wondering what difference one particular child in my class would make in my life.

Carolyn was an exceptionally bright child, whom I encouraged the administration to let enter my class even though she would be a year ahead. She was transferred on a trial basis. Carolyn flourished, and her mother was grateful for my intervention.

Two years later, when I was no longer teaching at Phil-Mont, I heard that Carolyn had been diagnosed with a brain tumor. I called her mother, expressed my concern and my hopes for Carolyn's full recovery, and closed the call by asking if there was anything I could do to help. By this time, Jim was ordained and the pastor of a church twenty miles away. While I meant what I offered, I didn't imagine I could much do from that distance.

In an attempt to stem the cancerous growth, Carolyn's eye had been removed, so she would miss months of school. She needed homebound teaching, by someone who had a Pennsylvania state certificate, and Mrs. Brown asked if I could fill that role. It meant adding a forty-mile round trip, twice a week, to my commitments as mother and pastor's wife.

Yet how could I say "no" to a request for helping a child who had already lost so much, especially one facing such a dim future? I accepted the challenge and was relieved to find that I would be paid by the state for my time and mileage.

I was even more relieved to remember the training God had provided for me many years ago, in those hours of tutoring I had once thought inconsequential. I had taught reading to a little girl who was going blind, racing against the time her reading would have to come through her fingertips.

Together, Carolyn and I studied history, English, and the Bible. Our sessions often included discussions of how the martyrs faced death, what made missionaries seek to go to countries of danger, and how she might face the unknowns in her own life.

Before we knew it, six months had gone by and Carolyn, while not progressing physically, had become more and more certain in her faith. She was ready to face whatever lay ahead. Mrs. Brown had become Charlotte, and our friendship was firmly established.

There was only one small hitch in the whole arrangement; every time I sent my forms for payment into the state, they got lost in some black hole. Multiple phone calls yielded no results— no acknowledgement that I existed or was on their payroll, nor reimbursement of any kind.

Carolyn worsened and died. It had been a long, hard battle for her, but her future was secure, and I could relax now that she was with the greatest of all teachers. I was glad that the friendship her mother and I had developed would help ease the pain of losing a daughter. As we shared happy memories and the sadness and grief that go with loss, I never mentioned the lack of pay.

When the state decided that the only thing to do was to start over and resubmit all of my paperwork, it meant that all my hours would have to be verified by Charlotte. The thought of asking a grieving parent to review and certify a sheaf of papers seemed neither compassionate nor appropriate. Instead, I accepted the invitation to sing at Carolyn's memorial service. As I sang "Be still, my soul …," I told the Lord that the money owed me (a few thousand dollars) was his. Money, no matter how much, was not worth adding grief to anyone's heart.

At that point, I could see only the confusing threads on the back of the tapestry; the picture had not yet emerged.

Eight years went by, and Charlotte and I enjoyed a close friendship, the kind in which all of the deepest concerns and joys of life are shared. Over lunch, I told her that church parishioners, and then others they told, were seeking my help with their family problems. I was being asked for counsel in their marriages and child-rearing problems: a bulimic child, an alcoholic husband, a teenager using drugs, a young girl having premarital sex, and a mother dealing with the belated effects of an abortion early in her life.

It was becoming overwhelming, and I was not certified as a therapist. Undergraduate psychology had not prepared me for dealing with such problems. Charlotte listened and prayed for me, good and faithful friend that she was.

Months passed, and one evening Charlotte called to ask, "Lois, how much did you get paid when you were tutoring Carolyn? One of my friends is contemplating doing likewise and is wondering if it's financially worthwhile." I stammered a bit, replying that it had been many years ago and the pay scale had no doubt changed. Knowing me well by now, Charlotte asked directly, "Lois, *were* you paid?"

When in a corner, truth will out. The whole story emerged, and then I held the phone away as she erupted in concern and disbelief. On a calming note, I assured her that the matter had been turned over to the Lord and had become only an amusing memory.

Charlotte evidently saw it as no laughing matter, for a few weeks later I received a kind note which expressed her regret that I had not been paid. A sizeable check was enclosed. Because three of our children were attending college at that time, Charlotte stipulated that her gift was to be spent only for *my* education—toward an advanced degree in counseling psychology.

After completing two courses, another note followed, this time with a larger check and the news that she would be underwriting my entire degree! Her gratefulness for what had been done for Carolyn knew no bounds, and my gratefulness for her warm generosity was exceeded only by my gratefulness to God. He had started weaving my tapestry years before, when I thought it was *my* idea to choose psychology courses to get me into medical school.

At age forty-eight, in a classroom of twenty-two year olds, not quite certain that my brain cells were still in working order, I looked at their young, inexperienced faces. "Whatever am I doing here?" This was going to take more courage than anticipated. Sighing, I heard the Lord whisper, "Lois, you always wanted to heal people. So you will, but it will be their emotions, not their bodies."

God had just turned part of the tapestry over, and suddenly I could see the Creator's design. This had been his plan all along! He had honored my obedience. God had never forgotten me or my dream; in fact, he had arranged and provided for its fulfillment. How did he come up with anything so perfect? I was breathless.

In addition, he was presenting me a means to provide for our children's remaining college tuitions. Now I had to see whether I could attain the grades that this opportunity deserved, by jogging my brain cells back into functioning!

They jogged quickly when the professor began class by making the statement that, as therapists, we should always begin with what the client presents. For example, if the client says "black is white," we should start with that premise. That statement didn't sit well with me, especially just after hearing from the Almighty. Forgetting classroom protocol after all those years, I exploded with a "Whoa!" that shook the class. I hastened to explain that black was never white, or vice versa, and asked, "Whatever happened to truth?" With great condescension, the professor responded, "Just who is going to *determine* truth? *You?*"

Now there are times when I just don't know to stop, so I replied, "Oh, I wouldn't *deign* to determine truth. How about *God?*" Gasps all over the classroom were audible; the "G" word had just been uttered! The professor's response was immediate: "Mrs. Caldwell, please see me after class."

Oh my, we were off to a good start. I hadn't been in class for five minutes and was going to the principal's office! Feeling six years old, I approached his desk after class. The ensuing discussion revealed that this master's degree in psychology was going to be a more interesting challenge than I had anticipated.

In those few minutes that followed, he asserted that God only existed because I believed in him. I assured my professor that even if no one ever believed in God, he would still exist. For good measure, I added that this was definitely not just belief, but my certain knowledge.

The man just didn't know to whom he was talking. I had been taught in the school of God's provision, his care, his plan for my life, obedience to his will, and his absolute sovereignty. Our discussion concluded by me suggesting to my professor that he just might want to find out if God really did exist. I must have spoken with the authority of someone who knew absolute and non-negotiable facts, for there was a healthy respect for my views from then on. We had many more interesting discussions in the following five years and, to my surprised delight, I finished every one of his courses with an A!

By my graduation, enough clients were coming to me that I had a full practice—an unusual situation, as graduates usually spend three to five years building a client base. It was clear by then that, without advertising or seeking clients, God was going to bring those he wanted me to help. Therefore, I settled into my new profession with the sense of relief and peace that this was God's work, and I was only to be his instrument.

This would not be a matter of doing things by the book and the procedures I had been taught, although they were often helpful. It would mean listening to the counsel of the Holy Spirit and doing things his way.

I marveled at how the Lord had prepared me to embrace this approach. In one of my courses in undergraduate school, we had used a textbook in which the longest chapter was entitled, "Jesus, The Greatest Applied Psychologist."[1] It had a tremendous effect on my thinking, and closer study of the Gospels has confirmed that title to be absolutely accurate.

There was value in searching the Scriptures to find the answers that would bring healing, for they were all there if one would search diligently. Thus the lives of some of my clients abound with accounts of forgiveness, healing, and reconciliation—all basics in the kingdom of God. Their stories also reflect the constant ordering and intervention of God, as he arranges the lives of his children so they might find healing in a world that is neither friendly nor safe. As I look back over more than a generation of counseling, three examples stand out as the sweetest and most dramatic.

Standard procedure after a mastectomy includes someone from the American Cancer Society talking with the patient about her feelings and what to expect in the healing process. I was about to be discharged from the hospital, having just had a double mastectomy, when the surgeon inquired whether anyone had talked with me. No one had, either because I had merely been overlooked or it was assumed that a psychologist could process her own fears and feelings.

A few days later I decided that, if I were someday going to counsel someone in my shoes, it would be wise to hear what the experts had to say. I called, and someone came to the house. We chatted for about an hour, during which I shared what I did professionally. As the woman left the house, she inquired whether I would consider counseling someone who was terminally ill. I assured her that I would and then dismissed the inquiry as a friendly gesture.

It was not dismissed for long. The next day, at her recommendation, a woman called to ask if I would see her. She was in the last stages of cancer, expected to live only a few more weeks. The divorced mother of two small boys, her boyfriend had abandoned her when she was diagnosed with cancer, and she had no close family support system. She was fearful about the future, had been to see a number of counselors, had not found peace, and was asking if I could talk with her immediately.

I was still in my bathrobe and only a few days beyond my own surgery, so naturally I was hesitant; however, I couldn't imagine Jesus' apparel or discomfort causing him to turn anyone away. I agreed to see Jen, on the condition that my bathrobe would not matter.

As Jen sat down in my living room, her first words to me were "Why is God doing this to me?"—a question I have frequently encountered in my counseling. After listening to her fears for her children and about death, all understandable, it became clear that Jen had no relationship with the Lord or any church and indeed had never once heard the gospel presented in a way that she might receive it.

With some trepidation, I realized that I needed to address things head-on—both for her sake, as she had no time to spare, and for mine, as I didn't have energy for a long discussion. I told her that *God* had *not* inflicted this on her and that her illness was indeed not of God's or her own making, but rather the result of living in a fallen world. I explained that God's part was to uphold her, provide for the future of her children, and take her to a safe place. As Jen left, she said she felt some comfort for the first time and asked to return the following day.

There was more talk about a loving God. Obviously she had more to cope with than any human should, so in a burst of compassionate frustration, I asked if she wouldn't want someone to shoulder the load. Her immediate answer was that she most certainly would, if only she knew of someone. I assured her that Jesus would, if she would ask in prayer for his help.

To my amazement, she told me that she didn't know how to pray and asked me to show her how. A simple explanation, that prayer is talking to God as one would to a friend, and then a brief demonstration by me led to the most direct and heartfelt request for forgiveness that I have ever heard. I had not even mentioned that sin needed forgiveness, but Jen obviously felt that she should not ask for anything without acknowledging that she did not deserve such love.

When she lifted her head, she smiled and said, "I'll be all right now." She told me that she would take her boys to the seashore the following week, for a last vacation together, and would be in touch after her return home.

I closed the door and leaned against it. Counseling in a bathrobe? Bypassing all the intake procedures? The lack of an office setting? The caution to never talk about faith? This was not counseling by the book; this was a walk with the King of Kings!

Two weeks later, I received a call from the hospital. Jen had been admitted, was not expected to live much longer, and was asking to see me. On morphine when I visited, she asked me to read to her, because she was having trouble focusing.

Jen had been reading the Bible, and she asked me to read certain psalms. Here was a Christian, just weeks old, who knew *by number* which psalms she wanted to hear, something my own longstanding acquaintance with the Scriptures did not include.

She had settled the issue of who would care for her children after her death, but now her primary concern was who would conduct her funeral service, since she was not a member of any church. It helps to have a pastor for a husband, for I was able to assure her that Jim would arrange the service and preach a message that would tell others what she had found.

The next day, another call came from the hospital. Jen was not expected to live much longer, so could I come at once? I hurried to her side and quietly waited, as she drifted in and out of consciousness. At one point, Jen haltingly told me that she was afraid to "do this alone." Never did I realize so deeply what "good news" means as when I told her, "Oh, Jen, we didn't have time to talk about that. You don't have to worry. Jesus says, 'Never will I leave you; never will I forsake you' (Heb. 13:5); 'Surely I will be with you always' (Matt. 28:20). And Jen, just think—you'll get to see him before I do!"

With those words, her smile lit the room as she quietly said, "I love him *so* much!" I took her hand and told her I'd see her again. Jen was with Jesus four hours later, and I'm sure of our reunion in his kingdom.

As we approached the funeral home, the parking lot was full, so we wondered just who this person was. We found that Jen had been a rather well-known artist, and the art community had turned out en masse. The funeral parlor was overflowing, with standing room only. Jim preached and told of Jen's joy in finding Jesus. She would have been pleased to know how her short earthly relationship with her Lord had reached so many.

That improbable counseling experience had led someone to the heart of God and allowed me to journey to the gates of heaven and peek in.

∾

In stark contrast to Jen, who knew nothing of God, Ray knew about God and at that point wanted nothing to do with him, at least from a counseling perspective. As he entered my office after a short wait in our living room, which doubled as the waiting room, Ray announced that it was obvious from the surroundings that I was a Christian. He let it be clearly known that he wanted nothing about Christianity in our discussion. I assured him, just as clearly, that I had no intention of mentioning it if that was his desire.

Just to make certain that he clearly understood where I was coming from, I explained that while I would not quote Scripture to him, the counsel I would give him actually came from the Bible. I made the analogy that taking a car to the repair shop to be fixed, and the mechanic using the car manual to troubleshoot, was much like coming to me as a counselor, and me going to my "manual" for my answers to repair a life. One manual had been written by the creators of the automobile, who had designed it and knew how it worked; the other had been written by the Creator, who also knew his design and how it worked. However, I would oblige by not mentioning the Bible and would give my answers in everyday language. We agreed, and on that basis we began.

After we counseled for several weeks, Ray asked why I was so certain that what I told him would work in his life. I shared from our family's experiences of the faithfulness and absolute power of the Lord to provide and of being blessed in proportion to our obedience to his Word. Ray listened and was fascinated, not by chapter and verse of Scripture, but by a living picture of its applied truths. After that, I scheduled his appointments last in the evening, so there would be more time to answer his questions about faith. Often a one-hour session would turn into a two-hour conversation.

Ray's problem was solved, so our counseling sessions ended. From time to time, I wondered if those discussions had meant anything at all to him. It is not unusual, when people's problems are solved, that the counselor never again hears from them. So I was surprised when Ray called a few months later, asking to see me right away.

I was astonished when he asked me to give him a Reader's Digest version of how to tell someone about Christ. His father was ill, hospitalized, and not expected to live much longer. Time was short, and Ray wanted to know that his father would be a resident of heaven. I assured him that I would do my best to provide what he asked, but would he please explain why it was so important for his father to be saved, when he himself had never wanted to hear about it?

A smile appeared as Ray explained that our many talks had convinced him of a Savior's love and salvation, which he had accepted a few months ago and now wanted for his father. I gave him a clear, concise approach and prayed with him that the words he spoke would not be too late and would be just the right bedrock for the road to heaven for his father. They were, and Ray's dad left this world with the assurance of eternal life.

Just as one client doesn't know about God and another not want him, there is also the one who knows him, but the hurts of life have overshadowed everything until the hope that once sustained is faded and worn. None is dearer than Sandi, who came for counseling with a legacy of hurt, emotional abuse, and rejection so great that even her identity was in a state of confusion. While at that time she felt she did not belong to anyone, Sandi knows now, without a doubt, that she is the Father's beloved child and will always have a place of belonging in my own heart.

She was born illegitimately, and her mother left her father when she was six years old. She had no contact with him until she was a teenager, and then she saw him only twice before he died.

Sandi felt that her mother truly hated her. There were no values or morals passed on—not even the niceties, like how to keep oneself clean. She never received a present, and when she sought just a bit of love by saving her money for Christmas gifts for her mother, they were literally thrown back at her. She could still hear echoes of her mother cursing her and asking what she was supposed to do with the gifts.

At age ten, she lived with her mother's sister, who was a prostitute. When her aunt's clients came, she found shelter on a mattress in a closet under the stairs. There she would read—to lose herself in another world and a better life. While in junior high school, she babysat for a Protestant family, who invited her to church. That opened up a job at a Christian summer camp.

A door opened to a new world when Sandi came to know the Lord. One opportunity led to another, and she attended a Bible college to prepare herself for serving in missions. While there, she even sent herself Christmas presents, so that her fellow students would not know her background or ask questions.

When I first saw Sandi, there was confusion, a wary demeanor covered the hurt and scars that lay under the surface, and trust in anyone was a scarce commodity. As I counseled her, I could not get out of my mind the pictures of the sad Christmases she had endured and the dream she had shared with me, of wanting a teddy bear but never receiving one.

God kept placing those pictures next to my own experiences. I had sweet memories—my mother sacrificing so we would have presents, the great big smiles that had met my gifts of perfume or a small vase, and the teddy bear to whom I had told bedtime stories and had cuddled as I had drifted off to sleep. Most of all, I had always been tucked into bed by someone who kissed me, cared for me, and loved me.

No psychology book contains a recommendation to share one's Christmas with one's client, but I was following God's agenda. Besides, I was convinced that the Lord's ideas went beyond offering just Christmas dinner. So with a deep breath and half expecting to be rejected, I invited Sandi to stay overnight Christmas Eve and share the day of Jesus' birth with us. Actually, I had more of a Dickens Christmas in mind than a spiritual one. My insistence must have been backed up by God's own persuasion in her heart, for Sandi accepted.

Never have I seen a face filled with more apprehension than hers as she stepped through our door on Christmas Eve. True to form, Sandi had brought gifts for each of us, which were quickly put beside the fireplace. Hot chocolate and conversation followed the church service, and then it was off to cozy beds, to dream of sugar plums in the glow of electric candles in every window.

As was our custom, I put a present on each bed, to be found upon awakening on Christmas morning. Before turning off the candles in her windows, I put a present on Sandi's bed and, as she was asleep and could not know of my boldness, kissed her lightly and whispered "Merry Christmas." It was God's kiss, not just my own, for one who had waited so long for it. I had no idea that Sandi actually was still awake, the importance it would have for her, or how she would cherish it so.

On Christmas morning, anyone could have gotten lost in the sea of laughter, gift giving and receiving, and the pile of wrapping paper. We loved Sandi's gifts, and her eyes almost looked liked she believed us when we told her again and again of our delight. But the wall between wariness and trust broke with her tears as she opened her last gift, the teddy bear for which her arms had waited all those years.

More sessions in the counseling room and more years of sharing Christmases together followed, but nothing convinced me that God's healing had occurred as much as the geode she gave me, just before she concluded our formal sessions. Still sitting on the shelf in my office is her gift, one side a rough rock and the other a multitude of beautiful amethyst crystals. She explained that she was the like the rocky side when we first met, and her life had now become like the side with the shining crystals.

The greatest part of her gift, however, is the love I still share with her and the love with which she cares for missionaries all across the globe, in her job at a mission organization.

There is now no wish to be a doctor. There is only the great appreciation that God has let me see the greatness of his caring heart. The pain of seeing a wounded world is deep and often more than troubling. There are times of wishing I were not so aware of the hurts and scars that people carry, but then I wouldn't be as close to God's heart or experience the joy of seeing Jesus heal and save. The sadness of not being able to bind up all wounds is lightened by the knowledge that someday he will. The occasional desire to be anywhere but hearing the sordid and tearful tales of those who sit in my office is tempered by the remembrance of my friend and the geode that sits on my shelf.

Admittedly, my counseling approaches are a bit unorthodox. But then, what would one expect when they are governed by God's direction, rather than by books and prescribed methods?

Even suggestions on how to start and grow a practice look pale in light of how God operates. I have never advertised, but I relax in the knowledge that God will supply. He will bring those he has chosen me to help. The faraway places from which some have come are remarkable: Arizona, Kazakhstan, Colorado, England, Nepal, Japan, and Ivory Coast. Just as God's interests are global, so he has made mine.

God's way of healing has been an adventure I never could have envisioned when yearning to be a doctor. But the most wonderful experience is following Jesus closely enough to actually see people through his eyes and heart. I wouldn't have it any other way!

CHAPTER 13

FLUNKING RETIREMENT

Ne'er think the vict'ry won,
    Nor lay your armor down;
The work of faith will not be done
    Till you obtain the crown.
           —George Heath,
              "My Soul, Be on Your Guard"

Since my youth, O God, you have taught me,
    and to this day I declare your marvelous deeds.
Even when I am old and gray,
        do not forsake me, O God,
till I declare your power to the next generation,
    your might to all who are to come.
                  —Psalm 71:17–18

W HEN JIM WAS hired for his first civilian job after leaving the military, he had been given his retirement date as 2001. We both laughed then at a date which seemed more out of science fiction than reality. Surprisingly soon, that date was upon us, staring us in the face and demanding that some decisions be made.

How had we gotten from there to here so quickly? Where had the years gone? Oh, we knew we couldn't run a foot race anymore, Jim's hair had turned from dark brown to white, our joints creaked once in a while, and standing up sometimes required a moment to unfold. My stamina was fading almost as quickly as the color of my hair. Jim, who could always pick me out in a crowd by my red hair, now lost me quite regularly, as I began to blend in with blondes, but somehow our inner selves seemed more vibrant than our outward appearance.

There had been a lot of water over the Caldwell dam: the Berlin Wall going up while we were in Germany, a baby born during our tour of duty there, four more added over the next few years, a call into the ministry, and the years of learning that God would provide. There had been a recalcitrant church and learning that God is present even in the midst of hardship. We had seen what great things God could do with hearts at Dilworthtown Church, especially with those who were willing to follow him to the mission field.

Then had followed ministry at Paoli, leading nine mission trips to fourteen countries, surviving a bout with cancer, seeing five children through their college years and weddings, and having both knees replaced. Throughout it all, we had moved eleven times.

Color television had made its appearance during our marriage, air travel had become as ordinary as riding the subway, and cell phones had become common. We had seen men walk on the moon and the Berlin Wall come down. Whereas Jim had once worked on computers that were as large as small rooms and required punched-card equipment, e-mail now could connect people anywhere in the world in seconds, and computers could now sit on our laps and produce things once not even dreamed about.

A heap of happenings had transpired during those many years while age was creeping up on us, but we didn't feel old. Now came the questions. Exactly when would Jim and I retire? Where would we live? What would we do in the years the Lord still granted us?

We reminded ourselves that the word "retirement" doesn't appear in Scripture. There was still work to be done. The venue might be different, but the urgency and need for workers was still very much part of the journey we were on. Yes, we would receive a pension, and Jim's days would no longer be determined by circumstances of a single daily workplace. Now all we had to do was trust that God would point us, once more, in the direction he chose.

Our two-story, four-bedroom house with the steep driveway would not be the best place to call home in retirement, no matter how lovely the view. Besides, it would be best to move away from Paoli Church, so both we and the congregation could start the new chapters of our lives afresh. That meant decisions about where we would go and what we could afford for a new home. There was a lot to consider.

In the spring of 2001, Jim announced that his retirement date would be September 30th, so there would be time to complete the job of training his replacement. Unknown to us, there was clandestine activity going on behind our backs. Knowing that Jim would be departing, church friends decided to give us a retirement dinner in June, when we would not be expecting it, rather than wait until September. Dick Streeter arranged to take us out to dinner and explained, on arriving to pick us up, that he had to stop at the church to check on something. My knees were bothering me, but, after a little persuasion, I reluctantly accompanied him into the building.

Dick proceeded to Fellowship Hall and began to open the door. Catching a glimpse of a gathering of people, I suggested that perhaps we shouldn't interrupt. It puzzled me why Dick, who usually was so aware of people's feelings, would proceed to throw open the door and leave me looking at the crowd. It was even more confusing when that large group, whose privacy I was trying so hard to protect, suddenly stood and shouted "Surprise!"

The blur didn't compute until I began to focus on faces: missionaries home on furlough, people from every mission team we had led, and the mission and evangelism committees. Then I noticed the decorations. This was in our honor!

There was one problem: Jim was not behind me! He had stopped to straighten a mission display in the hall and had missed the whole surprise!

When not successful, try again. Everybody sat back down and, as I was still trying to clear my thoughts, Jim came sauntering in. Everybody popped back up and "Surprise" was repeated. Jim's reaction was a typical understated response, "What's this?"

Our surprise was a night to behold and savor. Every table was decorated to the hilt with globes, "missionary barrels," and bottled water with humorous labels. Everything was a parody of what we had so carefully insisted upon for the mission trips we had led. There was even a pot labeled "fish and chicken stew," featuring a rubber chicken (including feet), to remind us of what we had eaten in Ivory Coast. Someone had dressed all of the puppets, which had accompanied us on those many trips, in native costumes, and a show was presented that made our sides ache from laughing. A more serious note was struck when touching letters were read from missionaries around the world, whom we had visited and who could not join us because of distance.

That evening was also when God began to unfold the future for us. As the festivities were drawing to a close, Dick rose to make the final comments and announced that we couldn't just retire; we should plan on doing for other churches what we had done for Paoli Church. As our minds were already overwhelmed by all that had happened, it took a minute to realize that Dick was saying that Paoli Church would support us for a ministry of helping churches with their mission involvement. Dick concluded by saying that he already had three thousand dollars pledged for our future work!

Knowing how Dick's nudges from the Lord resulted more often than not in reality, Jim and I knew that our future work had already been decided. What had begun as an evening of fun and love had ended in a clear call for our ministry to continue, though in a more expanded fashion.

It developed that we would be on the staff of World Mission Initiative of Pittsburgh Theological Seminary. Having limited vision, we decided that we would serve churches in the northeast USA, to which we could travel in one day. God had other plans, for the first church to ask for our help was in Michigan. We had overlooked the reality that air travel could get us anywhere in the USA in one day!

And so began a ministry that would take us throughout Pennsylvania and to Michigan, Missouri, Georgia, Tennessee, and California. It would include speaking to presbyteries, giving workshops at conferences, leading churches into sister relationships with congregations in Russia, and helping missionaries get to the field.

Our retirement was obviously not going to be quiet or sedentary. To underscore that thought, when I announced to my clients that I would be retiring and moving, most of them decided that I wouldn't be much further away and, if it was all right with me, they would continue counseling with me. Evidently our journey was going to continue at only a slightly slower pace, but the destination was still the same: the heart of almighty God.

What followed was the inevitable search for a place to live, with the hopeful thought that wherever we landed, this would be our last move before the final one into our heavenly mansion. For *that* move we would need no realtor or moving truck, a comforting thought; however, in the very near future we would need to find a new home and arrange for the usual moving needs.

Years before, Jim and I had discussed this and had put our name on the waiting list at a retirement village. Now, every time we thought about moving to a place where the average age was a good fifteen years more than ours, we felt like we would be buried before we were actually dead. It was a lovely place in the country and, as there were no apparent alternatives, we figured we would have to adjust our outlook and be grateful for what was available.

While cleaning out my desk one morning, I came across house plans that I had cut out of a magazine twenty years earlier. Every time we moved, I came across the plans and longingly looked at them, wishing that someday I could build a house to my own specifications, and then slipped them back into the drawer. It seemed that dream was never to be fulfilled, that I was destined to live in places already decided for me, from Army quarters to a parade of homes determined by calls to several churches. I had enjoyed those homes, but there had remained the dream of building our own.

This time I smiled sadly at the plans and dropped them into the wastebasket. As I cast a last, lingering look at that paper lying in the trash, I was even somewhat proud of myself for learning to let go of dreams.

Only a few days later, I answered the phone and found myself talking to one of our parishioners, who had recently moved. During the conversation, I mentioned that we would be moving to the retirement village when Jim retired. Agreeing with Joyce's pronouncement that we were entirely too young to be moving there, I explained that we wanted to be somewhere where the snow would be shoveled, the grass cut, our home looked after when we traveled, and the heavy work attended to in our retirement years.

That long list didn't deter Joyce. "Well, you need to come and look at where we live. It's an age-fifty-five-and-over community where all those things are done, and the place is beautiful!" With that she gave me the directions to the community, and I chuckled inside. What Joyce hadn't figured into the equation were very substantial realities: this was their second home, they drove cars that we only dreamed about, and they owned a sailboat that Jim could drool over! So much for her suggestion, as well-intended and sweet as Joyce had been! Wherever they lived, I figured there was negligible possibility that we would be their neighbors.

At church, Joyce asked if I had checked out her suggestion yet. I realized that the least I could do, in response to her concern for us, was to stop by and look. The development Joyce had described was in the early stages of being built. As I drove up to the sample houses, I was reminded of my childhood, when Mom often took us to visit model homes. Realizing that she had been dreaming her own impossible dreams, I smiled at how history repeats itself.

Wandering through the two samples, I dreamed of owning such a fine place. No one else was there except the sales agent in her office, so I didn't feel conspicuous as I stood in the well-appointed dining room and had a conversation like this with God: "Lord, it's beautiful. You couldn't possibly mean for us to have something this wonderful to finish our life, although I sure would like it. Please don't think me ungrateful for all you've done for us, but you and I both know this is out of our reach, so I won't wish for what I can't have. Thanks for Joyce's concern. Amen." As I walked out, I added "But if you should decide to give it to us, I won't turn it down!"

To reinforce my determination to not be covetous, I stopped in the office to look at the impossible prices again. Then, when I had almost made it to the door, the agent stopped me with the question, "Did you see anything you liked?" My answer, which surprised me by its frankness, was, "Oh, yes, a lot I liked! Just nothing we can afford."

Discussion revealed that there was a smaller model available, which had not been built as one of the samples. I looked at the plans. It was exactly what we desired: everything on one floor, two bedrooms, two baths, a garage, and even a full basement (which the retirement village did not offer). Jim would have a place for his shop and train layout, and storage would not be a problem. There was even a deck out the back, a happy replacement for the lovely back porch we would be leaving. Best of all, if we *really* stretched, we might even be able to afford it.

When I returned with Jim, to tour a nearly finished house like the one we desired, he was as taken with it as I had been. Then we were told that, if we would sign for the house that month and close on it before the end of the year, they would reduce the price by five thousand dollars. And a deposit of only one thousand dollars would set things in motion.

We picked the "perfect lot," where the deck would overlook a wooded area, and marveled that we now had enough to cover the deposit. Having money in the bank was a recent and happy experience!

That evening I came down to reality with a thud. Since we could not run the risk of having two mortgages, this was all contingent on selling our house within the next three weeks. How probable was *that*? Further, what was the chance that a buyer would purchase a house with a five-month wait, while our new home was being built?

As I explained all of the barriers to Jim, I could see the disappointment in his eyes as he, too, realized that we seemed to have encountered an insurmountable wall. While I was still adjusting my thinking to once again accept the inevitable, Jim reminded me of something. Several months prior, one of my former clients had told me that if we ever wanted to sell our house, be sure to let them know first. Wouldn't it be a good idea to call and ask if they were still interested?

By now the couple most likely had purchased a home. Still, Jim and I had learned to listen to each other, and how could I argue with, "What can you lose by calling him?" I left a message with his wife that we wanted to sell. I had done all I could.

An early phone call woke me the next morning. Yes, they would be interested. No, they had not bought a house yet. When could they come to see our home? *Tomorrow*?

Frank and Lisa came at ten o'clock the next morning, and by noon they had decided to buy it. What was more amazing, they *needed* to wait the five months it would take to build our new home! I recalled my Latin: "Veni, vedi, vici"; only this time it translated "They came, they saw, they bought!" Yes, God did want us to finish life in a lovely new home. He also had been quite thrifty with his (our) money—he had just saved the realtor's fee! Frank and Lisa were committed Christians whom we could trust, so no lawyers had to be involved. As Frank dealt with mortgage title offices in his business, even that was expedited for us.

Now we had the delightful task of picking and choosing all of the options. With the five-thousand-dollar discount and the realtor fees saved, we could actually have more than the bare minimum. It would mean an additional window that we desired, a slightly larger deck, better carpeting and cabinets, and the addition of a guest room built into the vast cavern of a basement we were about to own. We could even make some changes in the placement of a few walls. But the most touching moment was yet to come.

Jim's retirement day included a lovely reception by the entire congregation, at which he was presented a gift of ten thousand dollars and eleven cents. Much was made of the eleven cents, each cent representing one year Jim had served the church. Everyone laughed as Pastor Dick explained that, since Jim had always been so attentive to details, it was only proper that this final gift from the congregation be equally detailed.

As Jim accepted the gift, he profusely thanked everyone assembled and then explained how I had thrown away my plans for building a new home, laying down a dream in order to willingly serve him, them, and God. This generous gift would see my dream to completion! With that, Jim handed me the check.

With tears in my eyes and heart overflowing, I realized again what a loving husband and also what a loving Father I have. Jim had noticed the picture in the trash, but God had noticed also—and had moved a friend to call, a developer to discount the price at the very time we wanted to buy, and someone to purchase our house in the very tight window of time. He had eliminated realtor and lawyer fees to make this new house affordable, and he had balanced the cost of all those delightful extras to the amount of the check I was holding in my hand.

That last Sunday at Paoli Church was truly remarkable. We were commissioned as Paoli's own mission workers for our new role of helping other churches. At the same service, Kathy and Steve, our daughter and son-in-law, were also commissioned as the church's missionaries. They had been accepted by Christar, had raised their support, and had just moved to the Washington, DC area to begin ministry to the 120,000 Iranians there.

All four of us stood together to have hands laid on us, be prayed for, receive the congregation's blessing, and be sent out to do the work of the kingdom. I looked at the woman beside me. She also had let go of dreams in order to serve God's people and now was willingly bowing to her Master's will.

Not often does a mother get to share in such a poignant moment, but there was an even deeper meaning. Jim was retiring from the active pastorate, laying down part of his work, and here was our daughter picking it up. The mantle had been passed on. What we had desired, to minister to Iranians and introduce them to the love and forgiveness of Jesus, we had never been able to do because God had directed us elsewhere. Now, this day, this hour, we had come full circle and the torch was being passed. God had not forgotten; he had merely transferred the desire to the next generation.

Could my Father's love ever be outdone? Of course not! But there was one last chuckle God would have.

The day came when we were to make settlement on both houses, one in the morning and the other in the afternoon. Friends had invited us to spend two nights in their beautifully appointed guest house, before the moving truck would deliver our furniture to our new home.

After the two settlement proceedings, we went to our new house to put up window blinds in our bedroom and prepare for the movers to arrive the following morning. Not keeping track of the time, we worked until nearly ten o'clock without stopping for supper. Suddenly hungry, we decided to try the McDonald's in our new town. A hamburger would hit the spot.

We were the only customers at that late hour and, as we stood looking at the menu, I realized that our debit card was at the guest house and I had only a few cents in my wallet. Jim dug into his pocket and realized he was in almost the same predicament. Pooling our few bills and coins together, we stood discussing what we could afford, unaware that the clerk was watching. We picked up our hamburger, chicken nuggets, and tap water (our limited funds wouldn't allow for Coke) and sat down, just glad for a place to rest.

Surprised by so much change left over, we realized that we had based our order on the price of a "meal." I suggested that Jim get another hamburger. As he held out payment, the clerk said "Sir, it's on the house." A little dazed, Jim assured him he had enough to pay, but the clerk insisted. What he had seen, bless him, was two elderly people in old clothes, discussing how they could put their pennies together to afford a small meal. Without realizing it, he had put the final touch on a whole series of gifts from God!

When the incongruity hit us, of having just purchased a house worth over two hundred thousand dollars and being seen as paupers, we exploded into laughter at God's touch of humor. But it didn't escape us that, no matter how wealthy we appear to others, we are always loved paupers in God's sight, needing his grace and mercy. We have never passed that McDonald's without remembering and smiling.

Now began the real business of retirement. First, we were surprised to realize how much we enjoyed being around each other. What were all those stories about couples getting on each other's nerves? Maybe all those nights of church meetings and sharing Jim with the congregation were being rewarded by the time together that we had always desired.

What we really appreciated was that the ministry we were doing was shared. It was fun going to presbytery meetings together and planning and leading our workshops as a couple, and there was more than enough to keep us busy. We certainly were not going to be twiddling our thumbs.

Jim was and still is the presbytery's Global Mission Advocate and was chair of the Mission Beyond the Presbytery Division. I was an area chair of the Committee on Ministry, but the work that consumed most of our time was our service with World Mission Initiative. It has been so varied that we never have even considered boredom a possibility.

We have put together many mission workshop weekends for churches. I have led retreats, and we have trained and prepared congregations to send out mission teams as well as missionary families.

While Jim has always been known as "Mission Jim," several people have now dubbed me "Mrs. Mission Jim." It has been exciting, for we never know to which part of the country we will next be traveling. Helping churches form partnerships with congregations in Russia took us back to that land. Mission has filled our time, but not so full that we couldn't find time to start and lead neighborhood Bible studies.

All of this greatly amuses our children, who are sprinkled around the country, leading their own busy lives. If ever they thought that our phone conversations would more or less be recitations of our daily walks and vitamin pills, they have been sorely disappointed, but I suspect that they all knew us too well for that. It was one of them who laughingly pronounced, "You and Dad have flunked retirement!" We wouldn't have it any other way. We wouldn't have missed being this close to God for all of the riches and cruises in the world!

A few years after Pastor Dick Streeter's retirement, Paoli Church found that it could not maintain the level of support that they had previously given us, so it looked as though our wings would be clipped and we would have to drastically curtail or stop our ministry. Did God want us to stop? Was it time to sit down?

Why were we asking these silly questions? The task is nowhere near finished. There are still people who need Christ. There were no instructions to close up shop. So we prayed that God would provide. The old method always did work best.

As I was preparing dinner one evening, Jim shouted for me to come and look at the computer screen. When I arrived to peer over his shoulder, he was staring at our support figures. Twenty-five hundred dollars had just been donated by a friend, bringing us up to the full amount needed!

Our work goes on. We have "flunked retirement," so I suspect that God has not decided we are too old. Our hearts still seek him and resonate with Paul: "if only I may finish the race and complete the task the Lord Jesus has given me to do—the task of testifying to the gospel of God's grace" (Acts 20:24). After all, there will be eternity for doing other things, but we have only this life to do the things here that are so important to God. Alvin A. Rusmussen said it the way I would have liked to:

> Arise! And give what you have left
> To make Christ known to souls bereft.
> His hand leads on, pray follow fast,
> The time grows short, then Heav'n at last.[1]

CHAPTER 14

TURNING
THE TAPESTRY

He leadeth me, O blessed thought!
O words with heav'nly comfort fraught!
Whate'er I do, where'er I be,
Still 'tis God's hand that leadeth me.
            —Joseph H. Gilmore

Remember the former things, those of long ago;
    I am God, and there is no other;
    I am God, and there is none like me.
I make known the end from the beginning,
    from ancient times, what is still to come.
                            —Isaiah 46:9–10

IN RETIREMENT, WHEN one has more time to ponder, it's
easy to let thoughts meander to wondering how we got from
there to here, from where we started to where we find ourselves
presently. Musing produces questions. "Why did this have to
happen the way it did?" "Why did it even have to happen at all?"
"Why did my road have to have this many twists and turns?"

Once in while God turns the tapestry over and lets us see
more than the jumble of threads on the back. He gives us a peek

at what the picture is becoming or a look at a section that he has just finished weaving. Sometimes he even delights in showing us his nearly completed work, to "make known the end from the beginning."

Scripture is full of occasions when God leads and then tells his people to remember what he did to get them to that point, as in the Passover story, told again and again throughout the ages. He knows we need to recognize his wisdom and power and be inspired to give him thanks and praise.

More than once, while knitting a sweater with designs, I have turned it over for a preview of the finished product and have sought out someone to "ooh" and "ah" over how far I've come or how well it's turning out. I could live without the compliments, but it's pleasant to enjoy my work with others, particularly with the one for whom the sweater is intended.

I imagine it's the same for God. He must enjoy watching us get from there to here and delight to see us grow and mature in trust and faithfulness. To be sure, some explanations he withholds. Sometimes we will learn the reasons for and effects of our journey only after the tapestry is finished, when it will hang in the mansion Jesus has promised us.

Happily, there have been a few segments of our journey where he has chosen to reveal the whys and wherefores. He has let us see the reasons for what we questioned, for what we thought were mistakes along the way, for the detours, and for what we didn't even know was involved.

Such was the case with our son, Dave. In Chapter 3, I recounted how, when Jim was called into the ministry and I was going to have to return to teaching to help support our family, I was anything but happy. Convinced that I obviously was the best person to care for four-year-old Dave, I was overlooking the truth that he had a heavenly Parent infinitely more qualified than I was. The importance of this was seen more than thirty years later, when I looked back over his life.

Donna Berger, who had volunteered to watch Dave during the first year I taught, never let Dave's presence interfere with her ministry of visiting the elderly. Enjoying those visits and becoming quite at home with the "lonely ladies" was a thread woven carefully into his life by the Master Weaver.

Just before Christmas in seventh grade, Dave's class was given the assignment that each pupil was to do something for an elderly person and then write about it. Since one of our parishioners was a widow in her eighties who lived down the street from us, Dave decided that he would help her with her Christmas decorating. With that in mind, off he went one Saturday morning.

When he didn't return by lunch, I called to see what had happened. Mrs. Clouser told me that she and Dave had been up in the attic, reading and laughing together over the cartoons in her collection of *Saturday Evening Post* magazines, which were stored there with her Christmas things. He had been invited to stay for lunch—his favorite, grilled cheese sandwiches and cookies.

On arriving home, he announced that Mrs. Clouser made better grilled cheese sandwiches than I did, and perhaps it would be a good idea for him to visit her again next Saturday. Dave never missed an opportunity to eat, but I could see that he had already made a new friend.

Those Saturday visits became a weekly routine. Dave's grandmothers were both in heaven by then, but he had acquired a new grandmother. The bond became so close that when Mrs. Clouser became sick and went to the hospital, it was Dave who was notified rather than Jim, her pastor. Likewise, when the Clousers held their family reunion, Dave was included and introduced as "my newest grandson."

All this would have been blessing enough, but that spring Mrs. Clouser provided money so Dave could go to summer camp at Deerfoot Lodge, a Christian camp that specialized in outdoor living and wilderness camping. The resulting love of challenges—hiking, portaging, managing to survive with leeches, and surviving in the great outdoors—was another thread being woven into the tapestry of Dave's life.

In his senior year in high school, Dave's desire for adventure and his love for the Lord led him to seek a summer of missionary service abroad. He was accepted by Teen Missions International for the team going to Papua New Guinea, to help build a hospital there.

Before sunrise of the day following his graduation, Dave began his trip to the jungles of that faraway place. There would be a journey up the Sepik River in a dugout canoe and weeks of enduring blistering hot weather, exceeding the 110 degree mark, as they carried steel beams through the jungle and labored to erect the structure.

Dave returned with muscles I never knew existed, along with confidence in what he could accomplish. He knew how to work alongside others, to take the bad with the good, to endure mosquito and bug bites too many to count, and he had learned the joy of serving others.

It was no surprise then, when Dave attended Wheaton College, that he chose to enroll in Army ROTC. The preparation which God had carefully arranged came to fruition when Dave graduated and accepted a commission as second lieutenant in the US Army, as the vocation in which he could best serve God and others.

Those threads God had woven prepared him for paratrooper and ranger training and eventually duty in Iraq, where temperatures that soared to 120 degrees were no stranger to Dave. Neither were long, hard hours of work in less-than-desirable, sometimes dangerous situations.

Presently a career Army officer, Dave is firm in his belief that God will lead him through all of life's circumstances, that only doing his best is good enough for the Master, that serving others is a noble profession, and that looking out for others comes before taking care of oneself. And to think that all this began with what I had perceived as disaster! It would not have happened without my giving him into another's care, visits to "lonely ladies," and God providing a "grandmother" who supplied a camp experience that prepared Dave for mission work and ultimately for his Army career.

When God turned the tapestry over and showed me the threads he had carefully used to form Dave's life and character, I was filled with wonder. All of my good intentions and noble efforts could not have been nearly as creative or effective in getting Dave from that four-year-old to who he is today.

We have seen that God builds with bricks, one layer one upon another, bricks that at the time we don't even know exist. Such was the case with Jim's circuitous route into the ministry.

Jim was not yet three years old when he was taken to Sunday school at a neighborhood church. He loved every minute of it, and he was thrilled and proud when he was given a little blue ribbon to wear, which bore the words "I am Jesus' little helper." Somehow that little ribbon and those words were the beginning of a building process by God.

As a boy, Jim would never have considered the ministry for a profession, for he was so shy that just talking to adults was overwhelming, let alone preaching to a church full of them. Besides, Jim was exceptionally gifted in math, the sciences, technical skills, and detailed work and was regularly winning prizes in those fields. However, the divine builder was at work, and only he had the master plan.

God kept the money in short supply so, when it came time to go to college, Jim turned down a partial scholarship to MIT. Instead he chose Drexel University, where he not only had received a scholarship but also would earn money and gain experience in the college's industry program.

He entered ROTC only because it was a required course for the first two years at Drexel back then. Finding that military training excited him, he continued on in the program and found his voice on the parade ground, leading cadets as a company commander.

Now that God had the man and the voice to go with it, he proceeded to construct the framework for what Jim would preach in the years to come. The realities of winter maneuvers in Germany, living in a foreign land, and years spent in the business world as an engineer resulted in realization of the hardships of life, awareness of different cultures, and knowledge of the working man's daily problems. What better preparation for the ministry could there be?

A deep trust in God's provision, resulting from the many times we had wondered how we would survive and he had been there with the answers, provided subject matter and the ring of authenticity that every pastor wishes will underscore his sermons.

God's plan had been so well executed and carried out that, decades later, Jim looked out into his congregation and saw the pastor's wife who had been his junior high youth group leader. As she shook hands after the service, she explained that when she had heard that Jim was a preacher, she just had to come see this marvel. She told how she had often expressed concern about Jim to her husband and wondered, "What will possibly become of this young boy, who says 'hello' and 'goodnight' to me every Sunday and speaks not a word in between?" Now there is nothing Jim loves more than to speak, especially about God's faithfulness and Christ's changing power.

But one thread that had escaped our attention was the call Jim had answered:

> Send us anywhere, O God, only go with us.
> Lay any burden upon us, only sustain us.
> Deprive us of anything—save Thy Son, Jesus Christ.

Six years into retirement, as I concluded my Bible study one Sunday evening and was saying goodbye to the women, one of them commented about that call, which is framed and hangs on our living room wall. "Ah," she said, "that's quite a statement by David Livingston, isn't it? Those words are the lyrics of a beautiful song."[1]

With her brief remark, not only did we find out where the words of Jim's call had originated, but we also realized that God had even arranged it so the call that beckoned Jim into the ministry was written by a missionary.

∾

Likewise, I have seen how God has been at work in my own life, weaving what might have seemed disconnected threads into a carefully planned pattern. For me also, a seemingly unrelated series of events had carefully been designed by God. During my high school years, there was much interest in the relatively new United Nations organization. My high school decided to enter a state-wide contest in which students competed in their knowledge of the UN, its makeup, and its activities.

History had always been one of my best subjects, so I was asked to study for the exam and represent the school. I came in second place, with my eye more on the fifteen-dollar award check and a trip to the UN than on honor for the school or a great appreciation for the organization. I didn't think much more about the event, but it was entered on my records that followed me to college.

Shortly before Easter break of my freshman year at Beaver College, I was approached with a plea to fill in for their representative to the Model UN meeting, of delegates from colleges across the country. Beaver's representative, a history major, was ill. Since that high school prize was listed on my records, they assumed I was an expert on the UN.

Their assumption was wishful thinking. However, being loyal to my school and realizing their dilemma, I agreed to represent Beaver. Our college was to play the role of Egypt.

My uneasiness increased as I realized that, while I knew where the country was on the map, I was dismally unaware of Egypt's political stance. Not only that, but I would be debating with students who were political science majors and would be future ambassadors. I plunged ahead, giving thanks for my ability to study and memorize quickly.

The results surprised me. My performance was good enough that I was asked to represent my college as France the following year, the one year in which France had multiple successive governments. It was almost impossible to untangle the politics of the country, but in my naiveté I again prepared. Again, I amazed myself by a good showing among the delegates from those universities that represented the permanent members of the Security Council.

And so it went, with me getting more and more immersed in foreign affairs. I was asked to head the Disarmament Committee of the Model UN and then was elected to be its Pennsylvania state chairman, which required traveling and speaking at colleges across the state. What was an education and psychology major doing in the arena where future diplomats were cutting their teeth?

What's more, I was a woman in what was then predominately a man's world. Had it not been for Eleanor Roosevelt being my dinner partner for three nights in New York, I would have been certain I was trespassing on ground where no woman was welcome. It really was curious to me, but not to the One who had planned my future.

God was preparing the opus that would be the music of my heart in the years to come: missions. What better way to prepare someone for the global scene than to immerse her in the cultural and governmental study of the world's countries? What better way to prepare a rather timid speaker for giving workshops and teaching on the problems of the world and the need for Christ? While now I am focused primarily on *souls* in those countries we have visited and speak about, I still give thanks for the twist in my life which took me into the realm of foreign concerns.

What I thought was incidental and accidental, God deemed necessary. What I saw as a series of coincidences was carefully planned and meaningful. God had been building and weaving, and at last he showed me how he had accomplished it all. Amazing? Incredible? What fun to see the finished side of the tapestry and marvel that there had not been one mistake!

One of the most delightful stories of getting someone from there to here is Kathy's tapestry: the weaving of a profession, a call, and a love story.

From seventh grade, Kathy wanted to be a teacher in a Christian school, so she had attended Messiah College and become well established in her teaching career. More than anything, she desired to teach at her alma mater, Delaware County Christian School, but whenever an opening occurred, it was either at the wrong grade level or in the wrong subject.

Year after year she put in her application, and year after year she was disappointed. Not that she was unhappy where she was; it was just a dream she held and wished for in her heart. And so, after thirteen years of teaching, she again signed her contract for the following year.

Kathy had an excellent reputation, and the parents were glad she would be returning. Along with her wonderful reputation was a strong code of integrity; what one promised, one made good on. Therefore her heart sank when, just after she had signed her contract, she finally received an offer from the school of her dreams—which included a ten-thousand-dollar increase in salary.

She wept tears of disappointment as she wrote, declining this dream offer to honor the commitment she had made. Why, oh why had it turned out this way? Why hadn't the offer come two weeks earlier? It seemed that her life had taken a cruel twist indeed! And to add to her disappointment, she would have to work during the summer to make up for the smaller salary.

As the school year closed, Kathy asked a school parent, a missionary, about the possibility of a summer job at her mission organization. She responded that perhaps Kathy could be the answer to their need of a program for the children of the missionaries who would be there that summer for a conference. Kathy was offered the job, accepted it, and was introduced to the orientation class of missionary candidates as a member of the staff they would be seeing at headquarters.

It was not lost on the veteran missionaries that in this orientation class there was a handsome gentleman exactly Kathy's age, who was preparing for ministry to Iranians. It seems that the missionaries were not only adept at presenting the gospel but were accomplished cupids, as well. One couple invited Kathy and this young man to dinner, slyly arranging for them to be seated together.

Everything should have worked out superbly, but Steve kept a proper distance. After watching in frustration, one of the men took Steve aside and asked what the matter was, that a good looking girl held no attraction. Steve explained that he had understood that dating the staff was off limits. Assured that there was no such rule, he lost no time in asking Kathy for a date.

The rest of the summer was delightful, but summer ended and Kathy returned to teaching as Steve returned to South Carolina, to pursue his master's degree at Columbia International University.

That year Kathy was telling her students about the need for young people to enter the mission field and was lauding missionary work as a viable and rewarding profession. As she did, she recalled the children in her summer program saying that they wished they had a teacher like her in their overseas school, one who could make learning fun and an adventure.

It wasn't long before those pieces came together. If she was telling this to her class, perhaps she had better think about it for herself. This from the girl who had spoken passionately and loudly against going, when she was in sixth grade and *we* were considering foreign mission service! I do believe that God must do a lot of head shaking, chuckle at our inconsistencies, and have a good time changing our hearts.

Kathy felt led to take at least a year to teach in an overseas school for missionary children. Before committing herself, she joined Jim and me on our mission trip to Egypt. The trip settled Kathy's thoughts about mission work—a timely occurrence, for Steve proposed on Valentine's Day. This would mean joining him not only in his life, but in his call to work with Iranians. What had begun as heartache ended in the fulfillment of her desires.

They began married life at Columbia International University, where Steve finished his master's degree and Kathy taught at Ben Lippen Christian School—all with the goal of reaching Iranians. Today they serve the 127,000 Iranians in the Washington, DC area, reaching out, teaching, and discipling in Farsi. Their biggest blessing, however, is their knowledge that God has their lives firmly in his hands. He has built their lives together, cemented them with love, let them share in the joy of serving him, and blessed them with a delightful child upon whom to lavish the love that God has lavished on them. There had been no mistake.

Certainly God does not reveal his purposes for everything we experience in this life, but it is good of him to sometimes let us stand on higher ground—to see the finished picture of how he worked those events for our good. They have all been put in our path for reasons: to teach us, to mature our faith, to help us better understand him, to prepare us for his service, and always to get us to know him and enjoy him forever.

Perhaps the most profound lesson in looking back and seeing the path by which we have come is that, while Satan may be the prince of this world, the universe is still under God's control and nothing "will be able to separate us from the love of God" (Rom. 8:39). His hand selects and directs the threads that are woven into our tapestries, the dark and somber ones as well as the golden, shining ones.

> My Father's way may twist and turn,
>   My heart may throb and ache;
> But in my soul I'm glad to know,
>   He maketh no mistake
>
> My cherished plans may go astray,
>   My hopes may fade away;
> But still I'll trust my Lord to lead,
>   For He doth know the way.
>
> For by and by the mist will lift,
>   And plain it all He'll make;
> Through all the way, tho' dark to me,
>   He made not one mistake.[2]
>   —A. M. Overton

CHAPTER 15

STRAIGHT TO
THE HEART OF GOD

O Jesus, blest Redeemer,
   Sent from the heart of God,
Hold us who wait before Thee
   Near to the heart of God.
        —Cleland B. McAfee

I consider everything a loss compared to the surpassing greatness of knowing Christ Jesus my Lord ...
        —Philippians 3:8

SO HERE WE are in the telling of our journey—not at its end, but far enough along to see clearly that by following Jesus, we truly have been led nearer and nearer to the heart of God.

It takes a heap of experience to build trust. While harrowing at times, we actually began to see this life of faith and trust as invigorating! The more certain we became of the One who was making the improbable and "impossible" come to pass, the more exciting yet peaceful became the watching and waiting.

There was yet another area of growth as we walked the path of obedience and trust. Our focus was shifting from ourselves to others. As we grew in our confidence that God would take care of us, we became more open to being aware of what he sees and caring about what matters to him. This was truly a shift in thinking and focus—to seeing the needs of those in the world around us as clearly as our own.

What also became clear is that Jesus is often seen best through the eyes of need: the needs of people, the need for salvation, the need of our Savior's guiding hand through life, the need to have his blessing. And to think I had once hated the word "need" and had thought myself sufficient for any task! We finally came to know the wonderful comfort of being needy and having all of our needs met—by the most generous, loving hand that anyone can ever know.

Much is written about how faith can be increased. After all we have journeyed through, we have come to see the need is not so much for great faith, but for better knowing the great God who is always faithful. The real story is not about how we made it through, or the faith it took to come out the other end intact, or the wonderful adventures we had and continue to have, or even the marvelous blessings that were poured out in torrents. Rather, it is all about getting to know God, finding out who he really is, and seeing what his heart is really like.

Years ago, I was captivated by these words in Philippians 3:10 (NASB): "that I may *know* Him, and the power of His resurrection, and the fellowship of His sufferings ..." I pondered Paul wanting to know him. After all, didn't a man who had his theological knowledge know Christ? Like Paul, our following Jesus through the trials and wonders of life has brought us to know not only *about* him, as many Christians do and as we did when we started our journey, but to know him in the most intimate ways: his character, his personality, his love, his heart—and the things that both sadden it and make it glad.

The Scriptures describe God as the one "who richly provides us with everything for our enjoyment" (1 Tim. 6:17). We found "everything" to be true: plums, pruning, bicycles, filing cabinets, vacations, cars, houses, wardrobes, tuition, guidance, deliverance, peace, and hope. Even more delightful, he somehow had let us see *his* pleasure in giving it all.

When we read, "If we are faithless, he will remain faithful" (2 Tim. 2:13), we know it to be so. We had doubted, despaired, and questioned, and never once did God reprimand us or turn away. He was always right there with us.

We are told, "surely I am with you always" (Matt. 28:20), and Jesus never let go of our hands as he took us on the path further toward his Father's heart. Oh yes, we would have jumped ship many a time, but Jesus was there to pursue us, help us walk on water, and make the rough places plain as we gingerly made our way along. He kept us from sinking, either under the load of work that was required or the discouragement and worry that would sometimes assail us. He often lifted our heads to view a brighter future and took us where the waves were not as fierce. When we felt alone, he brought others to help us row our boat.

During bouts with pneumonia, earaches, cancer, and knee replacements, we discovered that he "heals all your diseases" (Ps. 103:3). He could and did come in the middle of the night and lay a hand on a fevered brow, and he gave songs in the midst of pain and assurance when we were troubled.

Of course we knew that he was our Redeemer and Savior, but we hadn't known how far salvation went. We hadn't realized that it was not only being saved to eternal life, but being delivered from doubt, from being too weary to continue, from our own desires and longing for comfort, and from our fears and selfishness.

As Jesus led us through times of hardship and joy, he displayed "his unlimited patience" (1 Tim. 1:16). We wanted deliverance *now*; we pleaded for an easier way. Then, when we did like some of the situations in which we landed, we would have liked to tarry for more than a little while! Had it not been for Jesus' patience, we would still be limping along, wallowing in the stormy surf of life, or snoozing in some sunny interlude.

Enfolded in the love of God, we are now as convinced as Paul that "neither death nor life, neither angels nor demons, neither the present nor the future, nor any powers, neither height nor depth, nor anything else in all creation, will be able to separate us" from that love (Rom. 8:38–39). We have found the heart of God to be the safest and most comfortable of all places. Total certainty that God can be trusted is something to rejoice about in this day of relativism. There really *is* someone who is absolute, fully dependable, and never-changing.

I think back to the first time I sang a solo. I believe now that the Holy Spirit arranged for me to sing what actually was a declaration of my future, both here and into eternity. At the time, I was too busy wondering whether I would make it through without disgracing myself, by forgetting my place or hitting a sour note, to consider the words I was singing and realize that they might be prophetic.

Of all the anthems and arias I might ever sing, none can quite as well sum up the days I have had with God and the days yet to come. Listen with me, as once again I sing the words.

> My God and I go in the field together,
> We walk and talk as good friends should and do;
> We clasp our hands, our voices ring with laughter—
> My God and I walk through the meadow's hue.
>
> He tells me of the years that went before me,
> When heav'nly plans were made for me to be,
> When all was but a dream of dim conception—
> To come to life, earth's verdant glory see.
>
> My God and I will go for aye together,
> We'll walk and talk and jest as good friends do;
> This earth will pass, and with it common trifles—
> But God and I will go unendingly.[1]
> —I. B. Sergi

It is sweet to contemplate that God is eager that he not be a stranger when we meet him in our heavenly dwelling place. If we walk with him here, we shall know him well when we arrive! Because we have experienced his provision, we'll have no question about whether our needs will be met in that eternal place. We'll be acquainted with his sense of humor and will enter right into the laughs we will share, as we look back at our childish antics.

We have seen his care for the lost and will not pause to enter into constant intercession for their salvation or to pray for those who falter along their earthly way, as we once did. We will delight in it all—and be awed by the scope and majesty of our new dwelling place, near to the heart of God!

Our journey has been truly remarkable, but there is no finish line at which we will count our laurels. There is much more to come, though given our ages, I suspect not much more here. We look forward to the eternally pleasant business of knowing even more of the unfathomable heart of God. What we have already found, having touched it here, having known it but a little, is worth more than life itself!

To know God's heart better in the time remaining here may mean giving up what we deem comfortable, walking on a sea where the waves can be rough and unfriendly, or traveling through uncharted waters. But our Guide will be faithful, there will always be the safety net of his everlasting arms, and the warmth of divine love will blanket against winds that chill the soul.

I am fully convinced that he will always answer just as faithfully as he has answered the prayer I prayed every night of my early life:

> Jesus, friend of little children,
> Be a friend to me;
> Take my hand, and ever keep me
> Close to Thee.
> —Walter J. Mathams

It would have been enough had Jesus just stayed close, as I prayed he would, and it would be more than enough if friendship was all that could be had in my relationship with the Lord of the universe. However, to those who follow Jesus, there is a more definite destination and purpose—that we may come to know the heart of God, which has no ending of glory, love, grace, and wonder, and of which we may partake for all eternity.

Follow closely! If you allow him, Jesus will take you there, as surely as he has taken us.

AFTERWORD

Turn your eyes upon Jesus,
    Look full in His wonderful face;
And the things of earth will grow strangely dim
    In the light of His glory and grace.[1]
        —Helen H. Lemmel

After you have had children and grandchildren and
have lived in the land a long time ... if from there you
seek the LORD your God, you will find him if you look
for him with all your heart and with all your soul.
                                    —Deuteronomy 4:25, 29

JUST AS I started with a word to our children, so I close with a
note of clarification to them and to all of you who have shared
in reading our story.

This account is not just the meanderings of memories or
humorous jottings from our journey. While it is to be enjoyed, it
is primarily meant for your profit, and it is intended to be shared
with the generations to come. Our walk has been a long one, so that
yours might be more direct and less arduous. We have encountered
heavy seas and hills and valleys. By hearing our story, we trust that

you will embrace life as an adventure leading to treasure which cannot be equaled.

Perhaps this book will encourage you to let go of worry and material things more easily, so you may trust God's enormous grace and provision more fully. Or perhaps, having read of the wonderful way in which Jesus leads, you will be prompted to revise your system of values so that self and pleasure, which seem to dominate society today, will give way to desires to mirror the character of God. And perhaps you will no longer define the pleasant turns of life as "lucky," but will come to know, as we have, that Jesus' leading has brought you to that place. Hopefully, you will come to define downturns the same way and accept that they are for maturing you and leading you closer to God's heart.

Certainly we could never have come this far without the help of many others, including all of you whom I've mentioned. Most assuredly, it was Jesus who led us, but the love, support, laughter, prayer, and encouragement that you gave so freely often lit our path, smoothed our way, and soothed our souls. You have walked faithfully with us as we've journeyed toward the finish line, and we love you dearly for it.

So it will be with each of you. Others will walk hand-in-hand with you, and you will encourage and love each other as you go your individual ways, but Jesus will be the most trustworthy and faithful companion in your own journeys to God's heart. Be sure to fear the Lord, serve him in all things, and share the great things he has done for us all. And as you remember the things of the past, look to the future, for it will hold the same journey's end for you—the heart of God.

Love and blessings,

Mom / Your friend

ENDNOTES

Prologue: PREPARE YE THE WAY

1. Lois S. Johnson, "Our Thanks, O God, for Parents" (Singspiration, 1967).
2. C. Austin Miles, "In the Garden" (The Rodeheaver Co., renewed 1940).
3. Philip P. Bliss, "Let the Lower Lights Be Burning."

Chapter 1: CHRISTIAN, LOVE ME MORE THAN THESE

1. David J. Mitchell, *A Boy's War* (Singapore: Overseas Missionary Fellowship, 1988), 139-142.

Chapter 3: MOMENT BY MOMENT

1. Annie Johnson Flint, "He Giveth More Grace" (Kansas City, MO: Lillenas Publishing Co, renewed 1969).
2. François Fénelon, *Selections from the Writings of Francois Fénelon*, ed. Thomas S. Kepler (Nashville: Upper Room, 1962), 15.
3. Brother Lawrence, *The Practice of the Presence of God* (Old Tappan, NJ: Fleming H. Revell Co., 1970), 61.

4. Corrie ten Boom, *Marching Orders for the End Battle* (Ft. Washington, PA: Christian Literature Crusade, 1973), 82–83.
5. Fénelon, *Selections*, 11.
6. Flint, "He Giveth More Grace."

Chapter 5: WHALE SPOUTS AND SHOOTING STARS

1. W. Phillip Keller, *Lessons from a Sheepdog* (Nashville: Thomas Nelson, 2002).
2. Miles, "In the Garden" (see Prologue, n. 2).

Chapter 6: MUSIC IN OUR HEARTS

1. Carol Owens, "Freely, Freely" (Lexicon Music, Inc., 1972).

Chapter 8: IN THE DIAMOND MINE

1. V. Raymond Edman, *Not Somehow ... But Triumphantly!* (Grand Rapids, MI: Zondervan, 1965).

Chapter 10: ANYWHERE IS TWELVE MILES

1. John W. Peterson, "Jesus Is Walking with Me" (John W. Peterson Music Co., 1978).
2. Bruce Larson, *There's a Lot More to Health than Not Being Sick* (Garden Grove, CA: Cathedral Press, 1991).
3. Alan Burgess, *Daylight Must Come* (New York: Delacorte Press, 1975).
4. Flint, "He Giveth More Grace" (see chap. 3, n. 1).

Chapter 12: HEALING HEARTS

1. George Crane, MD, PhD, *Applied Psychology* (Chicago: Hopkins Syndicate Inc., 1956), 628-655.

Chapter 13: FLUNKING RETIREMENT

1. Paul Billheimer, *Don't Waste Your Sorrows* (Ft. Washington, PA: Christian Literature Crusade, 1977), 130.

Chapter 14: TURNING THE TAPESTRY

1. Faye Springer, "Lord, Send Me Anywhere" (Musical Ministries, 1978).
2. A. M. Overton, "He Maketh No Mistake" (1932; by permission from Bob Overton, son of the deceased author).

Chapter 15: STRAIGHT TO THE HEART OF GOD

1. I. B. Sergi, "My God and I" (Austris A. Wihtol, renewed 1963; assigned to Singspiration, Inc.).

Afterword

1. Helen H. Lemmel, "Turn Your Eyes Upon Jesus" (H. H. Lemmel, renewed 1950; assigned to Singspiration, Inc.).

CPSIA information can be obtained at www.ICGtesting.com
Printed in the USA
BVOW031144041212

307201BV00001B/6/P